FLOWING

STILL FLOWING

Women, God and Church

Gillian Paterson

*The fountain is still flowing,
it has not dried up.*

Augustine: Sermon 315.8

WCC Publications, Geneva

Cover design: Rob Lucas
Cover photo: WCC/Chris Black

ISBN 2-8254-1312-7

© 1999 WCC Publications, World Council of Churches,
P.O. Box 2100 (150 route de Ferney), 1211 Geneva 2, Switzerland

No. 86 in the Risk Book Series

Printed in Switzerland

*for three beloved women who are part
of my own history:*

my mother Margherita Lucas Maclennan

*and my two godmothers
Joan Marguerite Platts
and Philippa Maud Robinson*

Table of Contents

Introduction

Women's role in society has been a key global concern of the 20th century. Gaining momentum as the century progressed, it has acquired greater credibility as more and more women have taken positions of authority and influence within the structures of public life. Even where pressure for change has been resisted, the women's movement has had an impact on human organizations in all parts of our world and in every walk of life.

Resistance to increased participation by women has taken different forms in different social, cultural and political situations. In religious circles, where the subordination of women is often supported by theological beliefs, the culture which endorses it has proved particularly intractable. For Christians, leadership by men may appear to be validated by the worship of a "male" God, incarnate in human history as the man Jesus. As a result, maleness has traditionally been regarded as a prerequisite for the administration of the sacred rites of Christianity. At the same time, access to *leadership roles* within the Christian churches is traditionally limited to those who qualify to undertake *sacramental duties*. This has made it possible for some churches and individual churchmen to dismiss the pressure for greater participation by women as misguided or even sinful. That position has become increasingly difficult to maintain in countries where the national culture accepts feminism as a legitimate human rights concern, but it still holds sway in more traditionally patriarchal cultures in every region of the world. Where there are few role models of women in leadership positions, the advocates of change have a difficult task in trying to persuade ordinary church people, women as well as men, that there is nothing unnatural about women's leadership or ministry.

It is against this backdrop that the World Council of Churches' focus on the participation of women in church and society must be seen. At its first assembly, in 1948, the Council received a report entitled "The Life and Work of Women in the Church". Since then, the "issue" has been on the agenda of every assembly and major meeting of the WCC.

It has generated a range of international reports and studies, of which the study on the Community of Women and Men in the Church was one. Most recently it focused in the Ecumenical Decade – Churches in Solidarity with Women (1988-1998). The culmination of the Decade was an international festival held in Harare, Zimbabwe, in November 1998, immediately before the WCC's eighth assembly. Attended by over eleven hundred women and one hundred men, the Decade Festival, with its combination of stock-taking and celebration, was the occasion for this book to be commissioned.

Going back fifty years, the story of the WCC's faithfulness to the issue of women's participation provides crucial material for any study of women in the churches during the 20th century. The Her-story project, prepared for the Decade Festival and the assembly, is an inspiring survey of the individual women who were part of that story – their extraordinary creativity, their faith in the future and the programmes and thinking they generated. In this book I make no attempt to tell that story. My subject matter is the experience of women over a twenty-year period, and the ecclesiological, theological and ethical challenges it presents to the churches at a particular moment in history, namely the beginning of a new millennium, with all the opportunities this offers for learning from the past and looking forward, in hope, to the future. When, one day, the dove flies out and does not return, just what sort of a community will she have found that is so good that she (or indeed he) does not wish to return to the safety of the ark?

* * *

Chapter 1, "The Road to Harare", provides a skeleton history of the WCC's focus on women up to the time of the eighth assembly. Chapter 2, "A New Community", explores the ecclesiological challenges identified during the closing years of the millennium, and points to their historical, theological and anthropological roots. The rallying cry for the

Decade has proved to be the question which the women asked each other on the way to anoint Jesus' body on the first Easter morning: "Who will roll the stone away?" (Mark 16:3). This text entered the consciousness of the Decade, creating a framework for the project of identifying the barriers to the more equal participation of women in church and society. The most formidable of the stones to be rolled away have been named as the poverty of women, the experience of women living under racism, and violence against women inside and outside the churches; Chapters 4 and 5 deal with racism and violence, respectively.

Chapter 3 proceeds from the question posed by Musimbi Kanyoro, general secretary of the World YWCA: "What did you come to Africa to see?" But because the encounter with Africa is not possible without also encountering its current economic crisis, because what is true about that crisis is also true of the economic plight of two-thirds of the world, because the wisdom and insight of African women have much to say to the rest of us, I have expanded that chapter to deal with the Decade's findings on the poverty of women generally, and the factors which underpin it.

In Chapter 6, I have tried to understand some of the discomfort experienced in church structures everywhere with women's sexuality in general, and to throw some light on the strong feelings aroused in many religious circles by the desire of lesbian women to be open about their sexual orientation. The final chapter is an attempt to draw it all together and suggest where priorities for the new millennium might lie.

A hermeneutic of suspicion
For me, the greatest challenge in writing this book has been the feeling – amounting to a compulsion – that I had to make sense in biblical terms of the issues I was writing about. In recent years, a wealth of scriptural material has emerged from the WCC's work on the community of women and men in the church. I was inspired by re-reading Wesley Ariarajah's brilliant little postscript to the letters of St Paul,

Did I Betray the Gospel? (Geneva, WCC Publications, 1996). I was spurred on by Musa Dube's extraordinary studies of the Samaritan woman and the woman with the haemorrhage; by Soon Ja Chung's reflections on the Syro-Phoenician woman; by what Ruth Muthei, Mary Getui, Pirkko Lehtio and the women of the Pacific region had to say about the story of Hagar; by writings on Jubilee and economic justice by Thaya Thiagarajah; by the Syrian women of the Middle East; by Ruth Harvey – and by too many others to name.

At school in Cape Town, I studied South African history. This started with the arrival of Vasco da Gama in 1497, and focused on the Boer War, the Voortrekkers and so on. There were some black people in the story, Dingaan and Mzilikaze for instance, but these were the villains of the piece, warriors who sought, wilfully and unreasonably, to block the expansionist ambitions of the settlers. I was almost an adult before I realized that this view had nothing at all to do with the real story of the peoples who lived in the region before the British and Dutch settlers arrived and who still live there today. Even sadder than the fact that I, an English child, was taught this version of events was the fact that the son of our African cook learned and internalized it too. To this day, I am no expert on the real story: the one I was not taught. Nevertheless, I understand from personal experience how powerful one's reading of history can be in creating and supporting national or institutional cultures. Therefore I understand enough to treat with grave suspicion any so-called history which is written by a colonialist culture and handed on to its children.

On similar grounds, I have learned to apply a "hermenuetic of suspicion" to my own reading of the scriptures. The writers of the Old and New Testaments were formed by their own societies, which were patriarchal ones. Their intended audiences operated within patriarchal structures. Where we find traditional interpretations to be hostile to women, or indeed racial minorities or other foreigners, we need to ask the following types of question: "By whom, within what kind of culture or structure, and for what purpose has this story been crafted in this way?" "For whom was it intended in the first place?" "Are we actually reading what is there?" "Are we suspending judgment on actions which should be judged?" "Why has this story traditionally been interpreted in the way it has?"

Under the influence of these questions, I was determined to incorporate a degree of scriptural questioning into the structure of this book. The narrative of Abraham, Sarah and Hagar demonstrates the way patriarchal systems treat women. But what does that mean in human terms? Are there moral issues here which go beyond what was sanctioned by the law? Beyond providing the teeming (or not-so-teeming) wombs which are the necessary engine of patriarchal history, do the women characters have an importance of their own in God's purposes? What happened to the teaching that men and women are created in the image of God? Eventually, I thought, "I am going to write this myself and see what happens" – thus underlining (though this did not occur to me until later) a central conviction of feminist theology: that experience, if not the sole road to truth, is a key *test* for truth and also a legitimate *means of access* to the truth.

Of the biblical episodes which come between the chapters of this book, some appear in the scriptures with male heroes or leading characters: in three cases, Jesus and his male disciples. I have reconstructed each in such a way that the main protagonist is a woman, basing source material on recent commentaries. The story which precedes Chapter 2 had a woman as the leading character in the biblical account, but church history has been written in such a way as to conceal the significance of that. Of the two Old Testament reconstructions, one is written from the viewpoint of a female victim of patriarchy, while the other is an interpretation of one of the few biblical texts in which a woman's experience of love is given as much emphasis as the man's.

I regard these reconstructions as a valid way of interpreting biblical texts, using the kinds of principles of interpretation set out by such feminist biblical scholars as Letty Russell, Elsa Tamez and Elisabeth Schüssler Fiorenza. Take the story of Abraham, Sarah and Hagar again. The original narrator had a number of purposes in relating this incident. There was the political agenda, the affirmation of the history of the Jewish nation, which had to be established at all costs. He must build up Abraham, the patriarch who was to father that nation. He was writing within a patriarchal culture which rejected foreigners, and had relatively little regard for women. Thus the principal concern in this narrative is for Abraham to have an heir, which he must do without too flagrantly abusing the laws of his people.

History and Christian tradition have done violence to the reputation of Hagar; yet the narrator is not unsympathetic to her. Hence it is possible to reconstruct the narrative with Hagar as the main protagonist, without substantially altering the original version of events. Where I have added detail, it is in response to gaps in the story which make it difficult to identify with the woman character. For example, the writer does not say how the Egyptian Hagar came to be a slave in Canaan; one of the forms of violence from which women of racial minority groups suffer, particularly against a background of slavery, is the suppression of their own history. But the most likely reason was that her impoverished family sold her for urgently needed money. This is something that happens in today's world to hundreds of thousands of daughters of poor families. While it does not change the story, the inclusion of such detail does help to make Hagar a human being with a past and an identity of her own.

Just as the Genesis and Exodus narratives are the history of a people, so the gospel narratives focus on the ministry and death of Jesus, this being essential core material needed by the early church. The main protagonist therefore is Jesus, the secondary characters are the male disciples or apostles. About all of these, we know quite a lot: their names, where they came from, whether they were fishermen or tax collectors before they joined the Lord. This band of men travels around Palestine, preaching, healing and generally doing good to a host of people, mostly nameless, normally identified only as "a deaf demoniac", "a leper", "a woman with a bent back" and so on.

We assume that these nameless people were not fictional inventions, as were the characters in the parables. They were flesh and blood individuals with names and families, financial worries, happy or unhappy marriages, rheumatism, leaking roofs or bed-wetting children. But we the readers know nothing of this, nor does it worry us as long as all we ask of the story is that it should tell us about Jesus. It was for this purpose that the gospels were written. The beneficiaries of his ministry were important only to the extent that they shed light on Jesus and his story.

It is important to remember this. It is not that Jesus himself was patriarchal in his attitudes or behaviour; in fact, he seems to have been singularly open to women, and accepting of their right to be equal participants. Nevertheless, in internalizing the gospel stories as the core texts of the Christian faith, we have also internalized what Elisabeth Schüssler Fiorenza calls a *kyriocentric* understanding of them: one that focuses specifically on Jesus-Lord-and-Master as healer, teacher, minister, saviour of a nameless and amorphous category of others, many of whom are women.

In consequence, the women who appear in these narratives tend to be the burdened, the sick, the sinful, whose relationship with Jesus is defined by *their* need and *his* giving. While male people were also the recipients of Jesus ministry, the response of male readers is altered by the existence of the category of male disciples, whose relationship with Jesus is defined by *friendship* rather than need. In failing to apply a "hermeneutic of suspicion" to this state of affairs, we may be giving biblical validation to many assumptions about women which, when we think about it, we know to be false. In particular, there are gospel women whose recorded behaviour can seem so extraordinary that we *know* there must be more to it than meets the eye. Why, in asking a favour, does the Syro-Phoenician woman behave in such a socially unacceptable manner? What would make an unknown woman with a doubtful reputation pour expensive ointment all over Jesus' head? Were they both mad?

So what I have done is to note how these stories speak to women from different parts of the globe – many of whom live in cultures with more similarities to the world of the gospels than my own – and to create a scenario which makes the behaviour of these women of the gospels a bit more comprehensible. From the perception that Jesus = Man = Master-and-Lord to the assumption that therefore Man = Master-and-Lord is but a short step. I have therefore attempted to retrieve their relationship with Jesus from the category of *kyriarchy*. To do this, it did seem important to give names to the nameless ones, but apart from that, the only liberty I have taken with the narratives has been to fill in the gaps, and turn "woman as deranged and nameless recipient of charity" into the more likely "woman who suffers", "woman who loves", "woman whom circumstances have placed under intolerable stress" or "woman who claims her rightful place in God's purposes".

In the case of the two reconstructions which focus on Mary Magdalene on Easter morning and on the reactions of Mary the mother of Jesus to the Nazareth sermon, a considerable amount is known about the women concerned. The task of reconstruction has therefore been rather different.

I have called all these reconstructed biblical episodes Windows, because they try to let in some light on the hiddenness of the lives of some of the women who people the scriptures, and to make sense of the way in which their stories have been told. Except for Chapter 1, each chapter is designed to be read in the light of the Window that precedes it. I have found that it is possible in this way to throw scriptural light on many of those issues around the nature of the community of women and men in the church which so trouble Christians today. The concluding Window, which tells the story of the first Christian missionary, points the way to an agenda which affirms the central position of women in the mission of the church.

It has been suggested to me that these reconstructions are too "post-modern", too "contextual", to be regarded as serious pieces of biblical interpretation, that their main agenda is to use the scriptures to promote a sectarian, politically motivated brand of feminism. I reject that view. The scriptures are not, in themselves, the words of God. They are written by human beings, peopled by human beings, and intended for human beings, all formed by and operating within particular contexts. Jesus himself, and none other, is the incarnate Word, the light that shines in darkness, revealed to us in the bonfire, the firefly, the lamplight glimpsed through a window on a dark night.

God and God's mission to the world are what the Windows passages in this book are fundamentally *about*. Elisabeth Schüssler Fiorenza speaks of the need to "exemplify the 'dance of interpretation' as a critical rhetorical process" in order to free the Bible from its patriarchal origins. This does not mean fictionalizing it. In many ways, the Windows are orthodox in their interpretation. Granted, the Window that precedes the final chapter (which concerns Martha and Mary) asks the reader to imagine an event which, on chronological grounds, could hardly have taken place. In terms of the interpretations suggested, however, I have not taken any major liberties which are not endorsed or suggested by mainstream biblical scholars. The subject matter of each Window is the nature of God: the triune, living God; the God who is always the same, always different; the God who draws each generation, each one of God's children, into that loving conversation which is at the heart of the Godhead, so that the world may be reconciled to God and to itself; the God whose living water is flowing, still, through our churches and through our world today.

Some words of thanks

My name is on the cover of this book, and I am responsible for what it says. It would not have been possible, however, without the inspiration, input, nourishment, support and midwifery skills of a host of women and men from all over the world. Aruna Gnanadason had the idea and along with Alexandra Pomezny and other WCC staff she has been a constant source of support and advice. In Harare, during the packed agenda of the Decade Festival and the WCC assembly, many people trusted me with their time, their thoughts and their experiences. Musimbi Kanyoro, Konrad Raiser and Irja Askola, though they may not have realized it, encouraged me to venture into new dimensions of "rhetorical space". Marlin VanElderen has been a patient, good-humoured and supportive editor. For four months, my friends and family have tolerated and defended my obsessive pre-occupation with the writing process.

I am particularly grateful to Michael Campbell OSA, who forced me to identify the criteria by which the biblical Windows might become disciplined pieces of biblical interpretation; and to Elizabeth A. Johnson, who gave me *carte blanche* to use her insights on biblical women. I found the trenchant comments of David L. Edwards most useful, and I have been encouraged by the interest and the enthusiasm of Lavinia Byrne, Sara Bhattacharji, Carolyn Newlove and Barbara Potts, and also my brother Keith Maclennan. On the Women's World Day of Prayer, when I was beginning to flag, the congregation of St John of Jerusalem Church in Hackney, London, revived my commitment with their delighted response to a presentation based on the central themes. Philip Pryke and his colleagues managed to take my house apart and put it together again while I sat writing away in the middle of it, and the community at Clare Priory provided a refuge during the dark days of February, when we were without heating, electricity, walls and, on one occasion, a roof.

But three people in particular have shared the journey and helped to shape it, and I offer them my love and thanks. They are Keith Clements, who has read and commented so helpfully on the text, both in sections, and then as a full manuscript; Ben O'Rourke, whose down-to-earth enthusiasm and personal support I have valued so much; and my husband Roger Feldman, on whom I have depended for his tolerance, for his belief in the value of what I was trying to do, for endless cups of tea, for running repairs to my technology and for asking the thought-provoking conceptual questions which, as an author, one dreads and longs to hear.

Gillian Paterson

1. The Road to Harare

It is being in touch with the big movement
which is the reality of God,
the wholeness of the universe in the Holy Spirit.
To do graciously, with deep meaning,
is theological understanding.

Lusmarina Campos Garcia, Brazil

Festival

Late November 1998. It is a hot, heavy morning, the sun bleaching out colours and pressing uncomfortably on unaccustomed eyeballs. The flame trees stand in black saucers of shade. Purple bougainvillaea drips from walls and trees, casting lacy shadows on the brown grass.

A white minibus swings into a driveway, past the security post, and draws up with a squeal in front of a long, low building which is the registration point for participants in the Festival to mark the culmination of the Ecumenical Decade – Churches in Solidarity with Women. Its doors are peeled back, and out of it clamber women. Clumsy from travelling, bog-eyed from too little sleep, they nevertheless have the surprised, expectant look that comes from arriving where you want to be but not knowing quite what to expect when you get there.

This particular group of women comes from Egypt, Sierra Leone, Sri Lanka, Britain and Romania. They have arrived on morning flights and been welcomed at the airport by teams of cheerful students. And now on the veranda a reception committee appears: more students, warm and delightedly helpful; staff from the Belvedere Technical Teachers College, where the Festival is taking place; Connie Mabusela, about to hurtle off to some further key task, who has managed the preparations locally and now has everything at her fingertips; and Aruna Gnanadason, executive secretary for Women from the World Council of Churches, based in Geneva. To Aruna, it seems like a miracle that this moment has ever arrived. Without the planning committee, without her wonderful and committed staff, without the personal support of WCC general secretary Konrad Raiser, it would never have been possible.

Belvedere's normal capacity is around 600 students, housed in long low dormitory buildings. It is being asked now to provide sleeping, eating and washing facilities for 1000 women and around 100 men. The past days, preparing for this invasion, have been frantic. Only four days ago the term ended, and Belvedere staff – from its principal and vice principal to its kitchen staff and the many students who have given up part of their Christmas vacation to be here and help – have worked day and night. Now, rooms are allocated, and the new arrivals sort themselves out, heaving or dragging their luggage between the buildings.

Arrival brings illuminating insights into the cultural diversity of the people here. Many have never been outside their own countries. Most non-African participants have not been to Africa before. For women coming from cultures where a high degree of personal privacy is mandatory, the warmth, openness and sociability of Africa is a new experience. In open shower rooms with tiny cubicles, modesty is next to impossible. College staff, it is said, went out and bought 100 shower curtains in the days before the great invasion. Alarming to some is the insect life, particularly a tribe of huge, crunchy flying beetles, rather like acorns, which crash blindly around until they meet their death in droves on the wash-basins or the wet floors. Belvedere kitchens have no experience of catering for a clientele which is not just international but also twice the size that they are used to. But through all this, the staff remain imperturbably helpful and tolerant, and by the end of the week it is difficult to remember the shock of the first arrival.

But now, on day one, there is still masses to do. An African village is growing up on the playing fields, thatched huts where the individual programmes and organizations will have the chance to meet people and present their materials. In the main auditorium, the "Her-Story" exhibition is going up, with its wealth of photographs and creative writing about women in the ecumenical movement. Pre-fabricated classrooms are being turned into bookshops or offices. The huge gymnasium, where the main meeting is to be held, is laid out with 150 round tables. Overworked staff are operating a drop-in badge-making factory, and working frantically to get photocopying and telephone facilities operational: so far, communication with the outside world is limited to a single mobile phone. Heavy storms are forecast – the elusive rains of Central Africa, a blessing really, but a daunting thought when one looks at the red mud and the spread-out campus. It is difficult to believe that, by tomorrow, it will all have come together. But, ready or not, the waiting is over, the sun is shining, the first participants have arrived, and the Festival is about to begin.

The WCC and women: a mini-history

For a almost a hundred years, women's participation has been an item on the agenda of churches, just as it has been in secular society. The issue has presented itself at different times and in different ways in different churches and in different regions of the world. The picture is not uniform, even within a single church, and attitudes at parish level may be more or less tolerant, more or less radical than the debates taking place in synods or councils.

In terms of structural responses, the pace of change varies from church to church. In some independent churches, and in the Anglican and Methodist churches of North America and Aotearoa New Zealand, there are already women bishops. Other churches permit the ordination of women to the ministry. With its increasingly organized body of women religious and lay women, the Roman Catholic Church is struggling to keep the lid on the ordination debate, but is being obliged worldwide to reassess the formation and participation of lay people in general and of women in particular. Many Orthodox churches, with their time-honoured commitment to their own traditions, are nevertheless exploring ways in which women can participate more fully in lay ministries.

The WCC has given priority status to the participation of women, and encouraged its members to do so too. In this respect, its influence has not been confined to member churches. In some national councils of churches (Britain and

Ireland, for example), the Roman Catholic Church is a full member. Even where this is not the case, Catholics have often participated at local level, and materials have gone into Catholic churches and women's groups. In 1995, I spent an inspiring day with the women of Mandragora, in Sao Paolo, Brazil. Set up to encourage and support women – Catholic and Protestant – who have done or are doing advanced degrees in theology, Mandragora has brought together Catholic and Protestant women theologians and post-graduate students in a new and creative sisterhood. On the day I was with them, they were responding to the Decade call to discuss the issue of women under racism. In that ethnically and culturally diverse country, it was a great privilege for me to take part in that conversation.

At the Amsterdam assembly in 1948, the newly formed Council commended to its member churches a report on "The Life and Work of Women in the Church". It was written by Kathleen Bliss and Olive Wyon and presented to the assembly by Sarah Chakko of the Syrian Orthodox Church in South India. Since then, the role of women has been on the agenda of every WCC assembly and has been a core area of the Council's work. Over the years, the level of participation of women in its assemblies, its advisory and governing bodies and its consultations has grown. A set of agreed goals for participation aims at a degree of equality in numerical terms.

In 1967, Brigalia Bam, now chair of the Independent Election Commission of South Africa, joined the Geneva staff of the WCC and took charge of what was then the Department of Co-operation of Men and Women in Church and Society. Brigalia moved the agenda on. It was not enough, she said, to limit "women's concerns" to questions of ordination and participation in the church. In almost every part of the world, women were disadvantaged educationally, socially, politically and economically. Since the attitudes and assumptions that underpinned that disadvantage were embedded in congregational, community and family life, it was hardly surprising that the churches, rooted as they were in their own cultures, were proving so resistant to change.

The focus of attention thus shifted from co-operation between women and men within the churches to issues of economic and social justice for women within society as a whole. The United Nations designated 1975 as International Women's Year, and laid the plans for its Decade for Women, which would run from 1975 to 1985. The WCC decided to sponsor a conference entitled "Sexism in the 70s", which was held in Berlin in 1974.

The idea of a WCC consultation on "sexism" was greeted in many quarters, Ghanaian theologian Mercy Oduyoye recalls, with "a lot of sniggers". What had sexism to do with ecumenism? But the churches were on the whole relieved by this new focus on economic and social issues, on development and human rights generally. "Women's rights" could be seen as a matter for society at large to deal with. Which was fine. *Of course* the churches were in favour of more justice "out there". The unnerving whispers of ecclesiological change could now be shelved in the interests of the *far* more important issue of the global phenomenon of the oppression of women. For the time being, the churches themselves were off the hook.

But not for long. While the UN Decade for Women did not specifically address religious groupings, the underlying social and economic issues identified at the WCC's 1974 conference were very much on its agenda. What would be a really distinctive contribution for the churches to make to it? It was observed that the whole history of theology and of biblical studies, which governed Christian formation and liturgy, had been created by men within a predominantly male ecclesiological and academic context. In 1975, therefore, the WCC assembly in Nairobi challenged churches to initiate and promote theological and biblical work focusing on the insights of women. Then in 1978, the central committee initiated a broadly based four-year study on "The Community of Women and Men in the Church", jointly sponsored by the Faith and Order Commission and by the WCC's sub-unit on Women in Church and Society.

The Community Study generated unprecedented interest. Its emphasis on encouraging groups to analyze their own local or national situation inspired many groups worldwide to name and analyze strands in the web of oppression which were taken for granted both in society in general and in the church. In looking at the church from within the disciplines of anthropology, sociology and biblical hermeneutics, the Community Study produced unexpected ecclesiological challenges and its report, received by the WCC central committee at its meeting in Dresden in 1981, gave rise to a heated and often angry debate. Some members found proposals that half of the persons on church bodies and delegations should be women unrealistic; some found it absurd to suggest that women should sit on the councils that decide the future of the church. Was it not time to call a halt to all of this and to recognize the right of individual churches to do as they thought right? The insistence that the women's issue is an ecumenical one was turning it into a major stumbling block to the visible unity of the church. But the Holy Spirit triumphed, justice won the day: a decision was eventually taken to affirm women as full and equal participants in the church, and to aim towards equal representation on WCC bodies.

In 1985, as the UN Decade drew to a close, the central committee received a report on its impact on member churches. It made for discouraging reading. Few churches had responded to a questionnaire sent out by the sub-unit to assess the impact of the UN Decade. It was clear that it had had little or no real effect on the status and place of women in the church. As one delegate observed, "In many churches, the position of women has not improved at all in the past ten years." During the discussion which followed, Methodist bishop Roger Uwadi from Ghana declared: "What we need now is a *churches'* decade for women."

A churches' decade

Despite statistics about women's participation, the decade leading up to 1985 *had* seen a growth of awareness in many churches of the obligation to give a voice to the voiceless. Many were beginning, uncomfortably, to look at the inequalities in their own ranks. The Community Study, in which

Roman Catholic women had participated, had provided the impetus for some initial thinking. All were keen to sustain the energy and momentum generated by the UN Decade.

So in 1987 the decision was taken to launch an Ecumenical Decade – Churches in Solidarity with Women, to run from 1988 to 1998. Its overall objectives were spelled out in "The Yellow Book", put together by Geneva staff. A key principle was that the Decade would belong *to the churches,* with the WCC's role confined to co-ordination and the sharing of information. The commitments asked of the churches included the following:

– to empower women to challenge oppressive structures inside and outside the churches;
– to affirm, by shared leadership, theology and spirituality, the decisive contribution made by women in churches and communities;
– to give visibility to what women think and do;
– to free themselves from teaching and practices that discriminate against women;
– to become more aware of racism, classism and sexism generally;
– above all, to be willing to introduce the necessary changes that would enable them to act in solidarity with women.

At Easter 1988 the Ecumenical Decade opened, with enthusiasm, high hopes and considerable media attention. Special worship materials were provided, including an Easter message announcing the Decade to be read at church services and other gatherings. Inspired by a Bible study by Mercy Oduyoye, the theme was the words of the women walking to the tomb on that first Easter morning: "Who will roll the stone away?" When they get there, however, the stone has already been moved and the body is gone. They are met by the risen Saviour, who says to them, "Go, tell my disciples..." And with this challenge the Ecumenical Decade was launched.

In more than a dozen African countries, national and regional events were held: processions, seminars and workshops, many attended by church leaders or even heads of state. Launch events in Asia included Easter sunrise services in Pakistan and the Philippines. In Europe, most launches began with worship. In Britain, 500 people attended a service in Westminster Abbey; the Methodist Church had women preachers at all its Easter services; and women's pilgrimages took place in other parts of the British Isles. In several Latin American countries, lively Decade groups were formed. Programme officers from 10 major US denominations formed themselves into a Decade committee, to co-ordinate resource materials and provide a unified curriculum for participating churches.

Given the insistence that the Decade should be owned by the churches themselves, it is not surprising that the local Decade was often not the same as the global one. Priorities and programmes varied from region to region. In 1990, Orthodox women from fifteen countries in the Middle East, Africa, Asia, Australia and North America met in Crete to celebrate the Decade and work out its implications for their own churches. In Romania, the Decade did not get going at all until the mid-1990s. In *Decade Link*, the WCC provided a focus for exchanging news, views, plans, theological thoughts, liturgies, hymns, songs and prayers. The Decade generated a wealth of creative and imaginative images, quilts, exhibitions, songs and poems. Perhaps the best-known image was the so-called "pregnant dove", given to the Decade by Eva Saro, an artist from Geneva – the Decade bird, hovering over the ecumenical boat, with the new woman in her beak and the world of the future in her womb.

Living Letters

Decade groups worked on a wide range of issues – war and peace, racism, the material poverty of women, health, violence against women, prostitution, the effects of displacement. Ecumenical theological and biblical studies groups – among them Mandragora in Brazil and Women in Theology in Britain – placed feminist approaches and interpretations on the map, boosting women's confidence for the struggle to become accepted in the still largely male world of academic theology.

Yet when regional delegates came together in Geneva to review progress as the midpoint of the Decade approached, the conclusion they reached was inescapable. In spite of all that was happening, the Decade so far had not produced much evidence of the *churches'* being in solidarity with women. Much more it had been a decade of *women* in solidarity with women, and maybe also women in solidarity with the churches. The main task for the second half of the Decade must be to offer its challenges *back* to the churches.

But how was this to be done? Questionnaires? Letters? Church leaders are famous for their overflowing in-trays, and the written word had not achieved much in the past. The apostle Paul had described the Corinthians as "a letter of Christ, written not with ink but with the Spirit of the living God, not on tablets of stone but on the tablets of human hearts". Why not try to organize teams to visit *every one of the WCC's member churches*? The teams taking part in the visits would then become "living letters" between the churches.

Approved by the WCC executive committee, this momentous plan proved to be one of the most successful and influential events of the Decade, not just for the women's agenda, but for ecumenical relations generally. Many churches had never received a visit from a WCC team. Nicole Fischer, who was a member of staff with the Commission on World Mission and Evangelism, and a former president of the National Protestant Church of Geneva, was invited to co-ordinate the programme. She says it ranks as one of the most exciting things she has ever done.

The make-up of the teams had to reflect "the community we want the church to be". It was decided therefore that each team should include two women and two men. One of the team members should be from the staff of the WCC; and another should be a woman from the host country, to help with matters of culture and language, to comment on the reliability of what the teams were told and to keep the churches accountable afterwards for any commitments that were made. In the event, these women found it extraordinarily empowering to visit their own national churches in the company of an international team, giving new and valuable perspectives on the churches and also their leaders.

By the time the Living Letters programme was completed in October 1996, some 75 teams, involving more than 200 people, had visited no fewer than 330 churches, 68 national councils of churches, and 650 women's groups and organizations. Very few member churches refused to receive a team. In the event, the only countries not receiving a full team visit were China, Liberia, Rwanda, Burundi, former Yugoslavia, Ukraine, Greece and Singapore, and churches in those countries were visited during the same period by a member of the WCC women's staff.

In every place the Living Letters teams met with church leaders, including patriarchs, bishops and presidents, and also ministers, congregations, students and professors in schools of theology. Precise agendas put together at national level responded to local Decade priorities, but all the conversations covered the four priority topics of the Decade: violence against women, women's participation in the life of the church, the global economic crisis and its effect on women, and the impact on women of racism and xenophobia.

In her introduction to *Living Letters,* the publication which came out of this four-year process, Nicole Fischer writes, "Many colleagues came back from the visits shaken by this first-hand encounter with the situation of women in the churches visited; all returned with tremendous respect for the often-unrecognized services and commitment given so generously by women." *Living Letters* sums up what the teams discovered:

– *Women are the pillars of the church.* Women love the church, they are the majority in most congregations, they are active in parish life through a wide variety of lay ministries, even where their contribution is not recognized and they are ineligible for leadership roles. At the local level, the life of many churches would grind to a halt altogether without the input of women. But they also met women who nurture a vision of a church which is a genuine community of women and men, accepting and hallowing their gifts, and proving a source of liberation for both. Sometimes these women have left their churches, if only temporarily, to start or join alternative church movements. The "women church", with its commitment to feminist perspectives and support for the community of women, is one such group.

– *Women are determined to endure.* Women are practised at endurance. They may stay married against all the dictates of common sense or self-interest. They persevere with children. They soldier on loyally in jobs which bring low pay and status. The teams saw many examples of such courageous efforts by women: women running rape crisis centres; national study groups and associations of feminist theologians; women's Bible study groups; women organizing community soup kitchens; ordained and lay women accepting the challenge of leadership; women breaking the silence, campaigning against violence or harmful cultural practices; women who have carried the Ecumenical Decade forward despite lack of support from their churches.

– *Women are forging partnerships with secular groups.* Many Christian women are active in the secular women's movement, and draw support and inspiration from it. The United Nations conferences of the 1990s, especially the Cairo conference on population and the Beijing conference on women, brought church and secular non-governmental organizations together around particular issues. Progress has been made in terms of increased visibility and confidence, the presence of women in the media, the acceptance of women as spokespersons for governments or commercial organizations.

– *Certain global realities are common to all.* The current economic crisis is producing poverty in all regions, North and South alike, with particularly damaging effects on the health of women and children. A further growing reality

is the upsurge in the number of ethnic and national con-
flicts in both North and South. Another is the universal
reality of multiple assaults on the environment, with their
threats of global ecological crisis.

When I asked Nicole Fischer what she thought was the
real lesson of the mid-Decade visits, she responded that there
could be no doubt that the Decade was having an impact. It
had served as a source of hope, a context in which women
could show their support for one another, an occasion for
women to speak out in the presence of team members and
their own church leaders, a catalyst for releasing new energy
for change, a trusted environment for sorting out different
understandings of the role of women in church and society.
The involvement of many men was another a hopeful sign.
Some, like Peter in the upper room, had said, "Supposing the
women are right..." These were men who supported the
process of women's journeying, who had heard their stories
and recognized the value of their contribution to the
churches, who were excited by the ecclesiological implications of the Decade agenda.

Sadly, she added, such men seemed to be in the minority.
Many leaders thought the time had not yet come for women
to play leadership roles in their churches. Many believed the
Decade was really a "women's thing". "There has been vir-
tually no change in theological education for women," said
Nicole. "And above all, while many churches believe the
position of women is a justice issue which the churches need
to tackle, there are still huge difficulties when it comes to
contemplating the ecclesiological revolution this will entail."

And so to Harare

So back to Africa, its red soil and its fierce if intermittent
sun. In her own way, in her own context, each weary woman
emerging from the mini-bus has trodden the road that has
brought her at the end of the Decade to Zimbabwe. Within
the ecumenical movement, it is the end of fifty years of
struggle for women – and the beginning of the next fifty.
What has she come to Africa to find?

She has come to find companionship, and a sense of a common struggle. She has come hoping to make sense of her own "Decade", and to relate it to the experiences of others. She has come with a strict agenda from her own church, or with no agenda from anyone. Perhaps she has little or no real expectation of a useful outcome, but is nevertheless glad of the chance to visit Africa, to have a brief holiday, to get away for a week. If she is not an African herself, she has perhaps come looking for the much-reported reality of that tragic and wonderful continent. If she is from Sudan or Congo or Angola, she may have come for a week of freedom from responsibility and happy worship, a brief respite from the barely-tolerable strains of living in a land at war with itself. She will certainly have come hoping for new energy to go on with the struggle in that long future which lies ahead once the Decade is over.

But best of all, she has come in the name of friendship: to renew old friendships and to create new ones. A woman in a red sari has been sitting on a bench in the shade, book in hand, peacefully watching the new arrivals. Suddenly, she comes to life. With a shriek of joy, she is on her feet, catapulting towards the van and into the combined embrace of the two Egyptian women who have just struggled out of it. It turns out that they had spent happy days together during a mid-Decade visit, parting – as one does – saying, "See you again"; and now it is happening. The Festival has begun.

Living water

An end-of-Decade event might have turned into a kind of wake. Instead, this was a genuine festival, a joyful, inspiring and ultimately hopeful experience, setting the seal on friendships, shared histories and the companionship that comes from being on a journey that unites women and men in every corner of the globe. I have said in the introduction that this book is not *about* the Festival. Nevertheless, for men as well as for women, as the new millennium opens, it is from the agenda and the spirit of this Festival that challenges for the community of women and men in the churches must be drawn.

Its most powerful symbol was the water. In the first morning's worship, women came, one after another. From five continents and 116 countries, women who carried water every day and women who had never done so their lives, in jam-jars and urns, bottles and pots, they brought water from their home countries. For more than a half hour they kept on coming, pouring their water into one massive earthenware African water pot, until everyone wondered if it could hold another drop. So the waters of the world, its tears of laughter and pain, its flooded places and its desert springs, its wells and its rivers and ponds and lakes were all mingled together in one place.

When the Festival was over, the earthen jar with the women's water was carried to the site of the World Council assembly by Brazilian liturgist Luzmarina Campos Garcia. There it stood on the dais for the entire twelve days. It is not possible to see the church of women as separate from the institutional church, or the church of the North as separate from the church of the South. The living water from Indonesia, from Rwanda, from Mexico, from Lebanon, from Canada, from Norway, from Papua New Guinea all flowed together into that one great earthenware pot. The living water may sometimes seem to be little more than a trickle: but it is there. It is women's heritage and also their gift to the world. The springs and wells from which it comes are still flowing. They will not dry up, nor the rivers turn back to their source.

With Fear and Great Joy

(Matthew 28:1-10; Mark 16:1-end;
Luke 24:1-12; John 20:1-18)

Miriam of Magdala, known as Mary Magdalene, is a leader among women.[1] Frustrated at the best of times by inactivity, she has just endured the longest sabbath of her life. Since they placed *him* in the tomb, a night and a day have passed, and now a second night is almost over: a time of the most terrible emptiness she has ever known. For the past three years, *he* has been everything to her, the community of his friends her family. Until then, her disability shut her off from all but her affluent, loving parents. And then came the day when she met him and was healed.

Mary has hardly slept. Every time her tired eyes close, the images come. Terrible images. *Him,* pitifully alone, dressed like a scarecrow, his face filthy with blood. *His* hands... she can feel the nails now, in her own hands, hear the thud of the hammer. *His* scream... Then the worst moment. The cracked voice rings in her ears still. "*Eloi,* my God, *why* have you deserted me?" For the first time, she heard from his lips the distant *Eloi* used in prayer.[2] "It's over," he whispered; and he was gone. When they took him from the cross, he was dead.

Then the hasty burial in the strange tomb. Watching with the other women, she saw the great stone rolled into the entrance. She longed to stay, to be near him through that first cold night of death. But darkness was falling, *shabat* was almost upon them, and she would have to go back to her people's house. It would be the first day of the week before they would be able to anoint the body and prepare it for its year-long vigil in the tomb.

In the dark, she can hear them coming: Joanna and the other Mary, competent women who do not fuss. It will be dawn soon, the waiting is over, and it is time at last for this final act of love. And then? The future without her Lord? About that, she is not yet ready to think. Mary collects the spices and ointments they will need, and together, their cloaks clutched around them, the three women hurry through the darkness to the garden of burial.[3]

The sky has turned to grey behind the still-black hills, but the garden remains in shadow. Mary knows the way with her eyes closed. Or does she? Something is not right. Is it possible that they have come to the wrong place? Even in the half-dark, she can see the tomb with its gaping mouth, the stone lying to the side on the dusty ground. Mary breaks into a run and, supporting herself on the rock, she peers into the tomb, her eyes adjusting to the blackness. The women step cautiously inside. The grave-clothes, folded neatly, glimmer white. The body, however, is not there.

Mary's heart stops. And in that moment of shock, the cave is filled with a blinding light and a presence, a voice that fills the tomb. *Why do you look for the living among the dead? He is not here, but has risen. Remember his words: that he would die, and rise again.* It is as if the cave-walls, the earth itself were speaking. Dazzled, terrified, the three women fall on their knees and cover their eyes. The great voice softens. *Do not be afraid. Go and tell the disciples that the Lord has gone to Galilee and will meet them there.* The light dims, the presence fades. But crouched there, clinging together in the shadowy cave, the women are conscious that a mighty power remains.

Their eyes become accustomed once more to the darkness, so much blacker now after the light. They are sensible women. They watched him die, they saw the sword pierce his side, they were there when he was buried. Dare they believe what they have just heard? They stumble out into the dawn. "That *was* what he said," recalls Mary. "Remember? That he would be in the tomb for three days and then he would come back? It means he is *alive!*" Tears gather in her eyes.

"But he can't be," cries the other Mary. "He really was dead. We were there: we saw it all." She too is weeping.

Joanna is troubled. "I do not believe it," she mutters over and over again. "And the others will *never* believe it. They will think we are mad."

When it is lighter, they check again inside the tomb, just in case they have been mistaken. They sit for a while outside, not wanting to leave this holy place. Then, as dawn advances through the trees, they turn towards the city.

But Mary lingers. It is a clean, lovely morning, the sky pink, the darkness melting to gold in the rising sun. She is dazzled by the new light. There is someone else in the garden, a man, his back to the sun, his face in shadow. A gardener, perhaps. For a moment, she is afraid. But he looks harmless enough, and vaguely familiar. "Why are you weeping?", says a kind voice.

Mary points to the empty tomb. "Sir, they have taken away my Lord," she answers simply, "and I do not know where they have laid him."

"*Mary,*" he says. Her heart leaps. It is *he.* Her legs give way beneath her. *It was true.* "Do not be afraid," he says gently. It is his own dear voice, embracing her once more as if he had all the love in the world to give.

"*O Master...,*" she gasps, reaching out for him.

"Do not touch me," he says. "It is not yet time. I want you to know that I am going home soon to my Father, who is your Father too, to my God who is also your God. You must go to my brothers. Tell them I will go ahead of them into Galilee and meet them there." He stretches out his hands, as if in blessing. And then he is gone.

Speechless with emotion, laughing and crying at the same time, Mary runs after the others. "Who was that?", asks Joanna. "It was *Jesus,*" she gasps. "It was the Lord!" She sinks onto a low wall, draws her cloak over her head and weeps as if her heart will break.

* * *

The next steps will not be easy. By the time the sun has fully risen, the women are knocking cautiously on the window of a little house on the outskirts of the city. The door opens a couple of centimetres and a frightened face appears. All eleven of Jesus' disciples are there, at what is obviously proving a difficult meeting. Mary knows them all so well: John, who was there at the cross with Jesus' mother, still wrapped in impenetrable sadness; Matthew, belligerent but resourceful; Thomas, pouring cold water on everything that is suggested. And Peter, usually so full of himself: she last saw him on the night before the crucifixion, chatting up a serving maid. She has never seen him so silent and withdrawn as he is today.

The women have planned what they are going to say. But in the end, they are unable to hide their excitement.

The words come tumbling out, they talk at once, their joy gives them eloquence in that gloomy gathering. The disciples are electrified by their story. In some, a wild hope flares; but they are practical men, most of them, and their principal emotion is disbelief. It is as if they dare not hope.

At last, reading the combination of hope and doubt on the familiar faces, the women stop. "Look," says Mary, "we *did* see him. The tomb *was* empty. There *was* an angel. We are all to go to Galilee and he will meet us there." There is a sudden silence. *They are not going to let themselves believe,* thinks Mary.

John gets to his feet. He has not said a word until now. "Mary," he says, "and all of you. Think very hard about this. It has been a difficult time. You have been brave, we have all said that. You were there at the cross when many of us were not. You saw him die. You saw them take him down. We know you loved him, and of course you are upset now. Well, we're all upset, we are all under strain. But we musn't let our imaginations run away with us."

James joins him, throwing an arm around his shoulder. "It's really dangerous to talk like this," he says seriously. "If the chief priests get to hear this story, there will be trouble. They are already scared stiff by the rumours that the Lord will rise again. They will think that we have taken away his body to make people believe that is what has happened. So you should be very careful what you say."

Nathanael looks up. "Jesus treated you as an equal, Mary," he says. "But everyone knows you cannot rely on women's testimony. You're more emotional and fanciful than we are. Not that you would lie deliberately," he adds hastily, "but sometimes women have difficulty in distinguishing the truth from their imaginations."

"You're right," says Matthew. "If it was really the Lord, he would have known women would not be believed, and he would have come to one of us."

The old frustration sweeps over her. Mary's fists clench. *Don't get angry,* she says to herself. Anger will make her irrational, and irrationality will confirm all their prejudices. "Look back," she says, patiently. "Don't you remember? He *kept saying* he would die, and then rise again on the third day. He said he would come back, and his spirit would be with us always. You *must* remember that."

For a moment, nobody says anything. What she has said is true. But these are men in shock. Whatever he said, he never meant it to be like this, of that they are sure. How could he "redeem Israel" if he were dead, or a ghost? His "other kingdom", where love and justice and peace were to be the driving force: they believed in that because *he* believed in it. But now he is gone, and the great adventure is over. To allow themselves hope would be to invite disappointment. *They are like sheep without a shepherd,* Mary finds herself thinking.

"Do you know," says Philip, miserably, "I'm not sure that I could look him in the face, after leaving him like that. We should have stayed with him. . ." There is an uncomfortable shifting. They are reluctant to meet each other's eyes.

"It would have changed nothing if we had," says James uncomfortably. "We could not have saved him. And he would not have wanted us to be arrested too."

Joanna looks up. "Oh no? Were you not the one who was going to sit at his right hand, to drink the cup of suffering he drank? Remember? That wore off pretty quickly, didn't it?"

James flushes. " What would you know about it?", he snaps. "Anyway, it was you who got us into that," he says, turning angrily on the other Mary,[4] "with your stupid ambition. And he blamed it on us."

"I know, dear," murmurs his mother. "I'm sorry. I didn't understand at that time what he meant by his 'kingdom'. I'm not sure that I understand now. But I do know that it won't be anything like this one. But this is not the moment to talk about it."

Andrew jumps to his feet. "How did we ever get into this?", he shouts. "We have too much to do as it is. These are *women*. Jesus talked to them like human beings, but this just proves that they are incapable of anything but tall stories and old wives' tales."

"Sit down, Andrew!", cries Peter violently. They all jump. "What if it is *true?* Let them *finish!*"

Mary understands their problem. Their entire culture has conditioned them to believe that women are incapable of sensible thought about theological and scriptural matters, that women should not initiate conversation, or answer men back. Of course she knows this. She comes from the same background. It was Jesus who made her believe in herself, in her own mental capacities and her own insights into people and into God. What a stunning experience – suddenly to be listened to, to know that what you think and say is important! But although this was good news for her, the men have never fully accepted that it is the case. Now that he is gone, she fears they will revert to type.

"There was something else," she muses. "He called you 'brothers'. He said 'tell my brothers'.[5] He never did that before, did he? He said he has to go home soon to his Father, 'who is your Father too'. So that *would* make you his brothers, wouldn't it? And us his sisters, of course. Supposing that is what the new deal is going to be: not that he leaves us, but that we all become his family, and part of that marvellous relationship he had with the Father. Remember how he used to talk to his *Abba* all the time? Maybe what we have to learn next is how to join that relationship as his brothers and sisters." She pauses. "It would be like being re-born, in a way," she says thoughtfully. "I think that is why we have to go to Galilee. So that we can learn about the next stage. It is more peaceful there than in Jerusalem – and safer too."

"Long speech, *sister!*" says Thomas sarcastically. He looks around for support. "We were having an important meeting when these *sisters* came bursting in. Enough of this nonsense! It's women's talk, at a time when there is men's work to be done."

From where Peter is sitting comes a muffled sob, a kind of low howl. "Did he say anything about *me?*" he asks suddenly. "Did he call *me* his brother?" He advances towards Mary so fiercely that she thinks he means violence.[6]

"The message was for all of you," she says gently. "You are *all* to be his brothers." And as she says it, her heart tells her that it is true.

"Then what are we waiting for?", shouts Peter. "Supposing he is still there?" Grabbing his cloak, he bursts out into the street and rushes like a madman towards the garden and the empty tomb.

It is the evening of that same day. Mary has come alone again to the garden of burial, the place where she met the Lord. Peter has gone, along with John, who came with him. She leans back, closing her eyes against the setting sun, replaying in her mind the meeting with the disciples. It was touch and go, she reflects. They are good lads, all of them, but sometimes she wonders if they have understood anything at all. Thank God for Peter, deep inside some private hell, who heard the message and believed. Peter is not someone she normally finds easy, but without Peter they might well have failed *him*.

For herself, she is filled with a confused happiness, which is very close to tears. He has been her life. He healed her, loved her, became her friend, and now, needing someone to trust with this astounding news, he has chosen her. *Thank you, Lord,* says her heart.

But Mary has learned something else from this encounter in the garden. She knows that the risen Lord, the one she must not touch, is now nearer to her than he ever was in life. For him, the agony is over, the nights of darkness have passed and the dawn has come. He is going home to his God, his *Abba*; back into the heart of that long intimate, loving conversation. But more than that. He is making a way for her, Mary, and for the others if they will, to join him in his love relationship with the God who not just his *Abba*, but hers as well. He is with her now, she knows it: with her, and in her, and all around her.

Mary also knows that being part of that conversation is not going to be something she can do on her own. For the little community of Jesus' friends, it will involve entering into a new kind of relationship with each other. She thinks of the men, their fear, their lack of understanding, their bickering. Where will it all lead? *I just hope you know what you are doing, Lord,* says her heart.

She looks up with a start. She could have sworn she heard him laugh.

NOTES

[1] Contemporary scholarship rejects the idea that Mary Magdalene was an immoral woman. Luke 8:2 describes her as one "from whom seven demons had gone out"; but while demons are associated with sickness, distress and seizures, they are not associated with immorality.

[2] Elsewhere, Jesus addressed God as *Abba*, meaning "Father" or "Daddy", not the formal *Eloi*, meaning "God".

[3] Some scholars believe that this anointing would not have been necessary after the "anointing" by the woman in Bethany (Matt. 26:6-13; Mark 14:3-9; John 12:1-8). Some kind of ritual embalming would have been normal, though.

[4] This Mary was the mother of James and John. The incident referred to is recorded in Matthew 20:20.

[5] Raymond Brown points out that this is the first time Jesus speaks of the disciples as "brothers", and suggests that this signifies that they are now to enter into a new and closer relationship with him and with the Father.

[6] We may assume that Peter was racked with guilt about his denial of Jesus on the night before the crucifixion.

2. A New Community

Our deepest fear
is not that we are inadequate, but powerful beyond measure.
It is not the darkness but the light that we fear.
Just look at us:
We are meant to share in the glory of God
and give others permission to do the same.
We have been given so much.
It is time to move on
from solidarity
to accountability.

Musimbi Kanyoro

From solidarity to accountability

"We have been given so much," said Musimbi Kanyoro in her opening sermon at the Decade Festival in Harare. "The churches, in us, have been given so much. It is time now to move on."

The past twenty years have left the churches with a possible agenda which spans a wide spectrum of their life. The Community Study, whose brief was to explore the quality and theological integrity of the church community itself, drew in local and national groups all over the world. Located within the Faith and Order Commission and linked with core concerns of member churches, it produced some profound anthropological, ecclesiological and scriptural thinking. The Decade has identified sources of violence and exclusion, and ways in which they are given legitimacy by church structures and leadership. It has also brought women together in *solidarity with each other* in a way that is new. However, the very words "churches in solidarity with women" risked giving the impression that it was setting women *over against* the churches, focusing on sources of division and alienation rather than on evidence of community. Located within the WCC's unit on Justice, Peace and Creation, its emphasis at local and national levels tended to be on activism and campaigning.

Community and diversity, wholeness and brokenness, reconciliation and confrontation: it is between these poles that all social organizations fluctuate. The purpose of this chapter is to sketch in some of the questions and challenges which they pose for the churches. Just what are the ecclesio-logical implications of the Decade, of the Community Study which preceded it, and of all that went before? In an effort to impose some kind of order on these thoughts, I have arranged them into sections dealing broadly with history (or historiography), spirituality, anthropology, theology and eschatology.

History, scriptural tradition and the apostles' apostle

The first Easter is the pivotal moment in the history of the Christian community. On that night, something momentous occurred, something infinitely mysterious which changed the world forever. But anyone trying to reconstruct the events of the following morning will run into problems. The gospel writers agree on the basics: the tomb was empty, Jesus and/or an angel appeared, the women were there first, responsibility for the mission of the church was then handed on to the male disciples. The first documented event in the history of the church was the commission by Jesus (or the angel) to Mary Magdalene (and/or a group of women) to go quickly and tell the disciples the good news of Jesus' resurrection. As for the precise order of events – exactly who did what and what hap-pened next – they all tell different stories. What is important for our purposes here is that both the founding vision of the risen Lord and his first "strategic instructions" were (accord-ing to the synoptic gospels at least) entrusted to women.

Summing up the study on the Community of Women and Men in the Church at the Sheffield conference in 1981, Elis-abeth Moltmann-Wendel opened a dialogue between herself and Jürgen Moltmann with these words:

> Church history begins when a few women set out to pay their last respects to their dead friend Jesus. It begins when, contrary to all reason and all hope, a few women identify themselves with a national traitor and do what they consider to be right, what in their eyes equals quality of life, namely, loving one who sacrificed his life, never abandoning him as dead. Church history begins when Jesus comes to them and greets them. Church history begins when the women are told to share with the men this experience.

If church history really starts here, she went on, why has Christian tradition labelled the resurrection story "the Easter appearance to the women", and assumed that the *real* beginning of church history was the commission of the male apostles (John 20:19; Matt. 28:16)? In challenging the scriptural origin of the church's understanding of its own history, Moltmann-Wendel is laying the basis for an ecclesiology which is radically different. What might it imply for the church to explore this other view of its origins?

Christian tradition has consistently underplayed the role of women in the gospel stories. Take, for example, the extraordinary liberties it has taken with the character of Mary Magdalene. I grew up with an image of her as a reformed prostitute, sexually enticing and perhaps a bit mad, whom Jesus, out of his (sometimes misplaced) generosity, had befriended. What seems to have happened is that tradition amalgamated a number of gospel women, and presented them to the faithful as one person. I have heard it stated from the pulpit that Mary Magdalene was the sinful woman who poured ointment over Jesus' head, the woman taken in adultery who escaped stoning only because of Jesus' intervention and maybe even Mary of Bethany.

I am not primarily concerned here with "what actually happened", nor with questions like "who was the real Mary Magdalene?". These are questions for history. The questions I am asking are about *historiography*, about how and why history has been written and passed down in particular ways. By what distortion of history has a powerful religious leader been turned into what US theologian Elizabeth A. Johnson calls "a beautiful, pliant sinner, symbol of female sexuality redeemed"? Biblical scholars today stress the lack of any evidence on which to base the assumption that Mary Magdalene was an "immoral woman". Nowhere do the gospel narratives show her as a prostitute, anointing Jesus or being forgiven her sins. Certainly, she is referred to as one from whom Jesus cast out seven demons (Luke 8:2), but evil spirits in biblical usage were associated with some physical or mental infirmity. There are no precedents for linking demons with sinfulness of a sexual nature or of any other kind.

Rather, New Testament scholars today agree that this Mary was likely to have been a leading member of a group of respectable women, some of them relatively affluent, who acted as facilitators of Jesus' ministry. In some passages she is the only person mentioned by name, elsewhere in the gospels her name heads a list of several women. The gospel writers take particular pains to stress the well-organized loyalty of the women at the time of Jesus' trial, crucifixion and resurrection, when the male disciples were in disarray.

I suggested in the introduction that it is important to develop a habit of suspicion when reading texts dealing with women. Can it be an accident that Miriam of Magdala, against all the evidence, has acquired this unpalatable reputation? Or is it that Christian tradition has somehow found it necessary to downgrade the significance of "the Easter appearance to the women" because of the apparent support it gave to the principle of women's leadership in the *ekklesia*?

Feminist theologians suggest three possibilities. First is the likelihood that men resented Mary's particularly intimate personal comradeship with Jesus; second, Christian tradition has been entirely unable to deal with the implications of a strong, competent woman, loved and trusted by Jesus and holding a leadership role among his friends; third, it was crucial for those who were responsible for the early church that the principle of male leadership – the apostolic succession itself – should be given the *imprimatur* of history. Here, say these theologians, is a stunning example of what happens when theology and religious symbols are crafted almost exclusively by men within a patriarchal framework.

There is considerable documentary evidence of a struggle within the early church in which Mary Magdalene was a leading protagonist. Extra-biblical texts such as the *Dialogue of the Saviour,* the *Gospel of Thomas* and the *Gospel of Philip* support theories of a rivalry between the male disciples and Mary Magdalene over her right to a leadership role. In the second- or third-century *Gospel of Mary,* the disciples, terrified by the death of Jesus, ask Mary to relate the things the Lord taught her when he was alive. They are at first interested, but then Peter interrupts in anger, "Did he really speak privately to a woman and not openly to us? Are we to turn about and listen to her? Did he prefer her to us?" Elizabeth Johnson, in *Friends of God and Prophets*, relates what happens next:

> Troubled at his disparagement of her witness and her relationship to Christ, Mary responds, "My brother Peter, what do you think? Do you think that I thought this up myself in my heart, or that I am lying about the Saviour?"
>
> At this point Levi breaks in to mediate the dispute, consigning Peter to the league of evil powers but defending Mary's role: "Peter, you have always been hot-tempered. Now I see you are contending against the woman as if she were the adversary. But if the Saviour made her worthy, who are you, indeed, to reject her? Surely the Lord knew her very well. That is why he loved her more than us." The result of this intervention is that the others agree to accept Mary Magdalene's teaching and, encouraged by her words, they themselves go out to preach.
>
> In a widely accepted interpretation of this text [it is suggested that] such second- and third-century writings use the figure of Mary Magdalene as a symbol for women's activity in ministry. This, it seems, was challenging contemporary male efforts, symbolized by Peter, to suppress visionaries and female leadership in the developing orthodox ecclesial community.

In the creation of history, the version which is passed down is usually the one which is written by the victors. This is not disputed today. In the case of these early women disciples, sidelining their significance has done violence to their memory and has deprived Christian women and men over the centuries of powerful symbols of female leadership within the early church. Object of desire, yes; sorrow for sin, definitely. "But," to quote Elizabeth Johnson again, "woman as creative leader chosen by Christ? Not likely!"

Spirituality and the rolling of stones

The story of the empty tomb has been a formative theme for the Decade. In her keynote book, *Who Will Roll the Stone*

Away?, Mercy Oduyoye named the violence and exclusion standing in the way of women's fuller participation in church and society. The mid-Decade teams and others have identified specific "stones" to be rolled away, notably poverty, racism and xenophobia, and violence against women (we will turn to these in Chapters 3, 4 and 5).

While church leaders are willing to acknowledge and condemn violence and exclusion when it happens "out there", it seems very difficult for them to face these realities within their own ranks or among Christian families and communities. Indeed, as Konrad Raiser has pointed out, it is from the patriarchal religious and spiritual culture of most churches that these abuses acquire their legitimacy. Patriarchy dates back to the beginning of Judaeo-Christian tradition. Abraham was the archetypal patriarch, Jesus himself a "son of Abraham", a bearer of the promise, with all the cultural baggage that comes along with this. It is not surprising that a couple of decades have not proved long enough to deconstruct a spirituality that is so rooted in the culture and history of most of our structures.

Nevertheless, in some places things have happened. There have been advances in theological education. More churches are ordaining women, and others, including the Roman Catholic and some Orthodox churches, are giving greater encouragement to the non-ordained ministry of women. But the major success story of the Decade has been the growth in solidarity among women themselves, who have basically said, "If the churches do not want to know, we will get on with it and do it ourselves." Many voices at the Decade Festival affirmed the importance of this crucial stage in the journey. Networks, international groups and the growth in trust that was so much in evidence in Harare are essential staging posts to the next leg of the journey.

Another hopeful sign is an increasing awareness on the part of men. In the past twenty years, many men have become aware of the violence inherent in male culture, its corrupting effect on men as well as women and the way the churches have condoned it. Konrad Raiser believes that the

Decade has helped to uncover defensive strategies and to challenge attempts at justifying them. The clergy themselves are representatives of patriarchal organizations. They may not like it, but there is no way in which they can disengage themselves from the structures. They have to accept responsibility. "We *are* our brothers' keepers," he says. Where women are still under-represented in church leadership (that is, almost everywhere), it is worth remembering that *many men do not want it that way either.*

To get another opinion on the Window that precedes this chapter, I showed it to a male friend, himself a theologian, whose views I trust. "What I would really like to know," he commented, "is what the men said after the women had gone." *That is for you to write, brother,* I thought. For con-scientized men working in patriarchal situations, these are difficult times. Living in the shadow of the moral high ground which women may occupy, they may still be thriving comfortably in the structures they are expected to deplore. As women needed to develop in solidarity with each other before they could go further, so men also need to learn from each other how to approach this reality creatively, how to promote the community of women and men in the church in a way which is better for all. So I look forward to reading this next scene, when it has been written by those who are much better able to record male conversation than I.

In summing up the lessons of the Community Study, Constance Parvey, the US Lutheran pastor who had WCC staff responsibility for it, said that "a significant faith disposition of those participating in the Community Study has been a readiness to live tradition as a life-style of anticipation rather than to see the past only as a burden from which to be delivered. The thrust has been not to dwell on what has not been done, but to concentrate on what can be done."

Contemporary management theory defines challenges in terms of barriers to a desired outcome. It defines the present as a set of problems, the future as a "solution" to these problems. We are asked to focus not on the vision itself, but on the stumbling blocks to its realization. In my Bible study group in Harare, there was concern about how the challenge "Who will roll the stone away?" seems to have dominated the agenda and image of the Decade. Certainly, it has been a powerful rallying cry, inspiring many to analyze their own context in a more disciplined way. Nevertheless, people felt that it was now time to move beyond its negative, problem-solving connotations. When the women came to the tomb, they found they did not have to roll the stone away. The living Lord came to them in person and said, "Do not be afraid." While identifying the stumbling blocks that stand between you and your vision is an essential part of strategic planning, it is important not to allow these lumps of rock to block the light. What is behind the stone is the darkness of the grave. It needs naming, it needs exposing, it needs to be engaged with, but in the end, our true spiritual home is in the light.

Jürgen Moltmann has spoken of the importance of distinguishing between the *anticipated* future and the *extrapolated* future. The latter is the future that arises logically out of the present, and the barriers to it are implicit in the current situation. The anticipated future, on the other hand, is that future which you long for, the vision which you write on the wall (Hab. 2:2). It is viewed through eschatological eyes, in relation to the time when all shall be made new in Christ. Ecumenical strategy, says Moltmann, involves living in the light of the eschaton, holding the anticipated future before you and then relating it to the present, from which all possible futures must ultimately grow. Activism, problem-solving and complaining are often essential stepping stones to where we want to be, but they are only stepping stones. Real progress, real change depends on the infectiousness of the anticipated future, the vision of the ecclesial community that will be better for men as well as women.

Anthropology and the wilderness community

I have recently been wondering whether Jürgen Moltmann's insight into these two "futures" should not be amplified in the light of the experience of more traditional societies, in which the *past* exercises a more powerful influence than it does in European culture. Belief in a future which is fully under the control of living human beings is very much a product of modernism and the European Enlightenment. Thinking globally, the quest for lasting change also requires facing up to the anthropological roots of the present. Unless the forces of tradition, the life-enhancing ancestors, the religiosity of the people are all able to come together in the task of anticipating the future, then lasting change will not bear fruit.

Religious structures tend to be particularly resistant to change. In any society, it is a small step from saying "this is the way things are" to saying "this is how things are meant to be" or even "this is how God made things". Thus scientific statements become theological statements, which in their turn become sacred norms which have to be defended by the church. The most difficult task for a Christian may be achieving a reconciliation between the eschatological vision on the one hand, and on the other, the voices of one's cultural, religious or institutional ancestors.

The discipline of anthropology was developed in the context of the historical study of ancient cultures, and applied to the study of so-called "primitive communities". There is a great need for more anthropological study on how churches handle change, and on the implications of change within the church community. In recent years, its insights and methods have been fruitfully applied to the dynamics of community and culture in the modern world, and the stresses under which they operate. The final report of the Community Study had this to say:

> We are seeking new forms of being together, but the old structures still exist. There is great tension between our dreams and our realities. We are experiencing different types of conflicting loyalties. Many times there is not room enough in the churches for the realization of our visions. Living between old traditions and new opportunities definitely means living in controversy. The ambivalence is not only an external matter. It lives within us.

Over the past two decades, theologians such as Hans Küng and David Bosch have been applying the concept of the "paradigm shift", developed by Thomas Kuhn in his *Structure of Scientific Revolutions.* There are some moments in history, says Kuhn, when the entire mindset of a culture is undergoing change, moving from an old system of beliefs to a new and incompatible set. Two examples are the Copernican revolution and Darwin's theories about the origins of species. Within something like fifty years, people all over the world moved from believing that the sun goes around the earth to acknowledging that the earth goes around the sun; from faith that all life on earth appeared fully formed about 6000 years ago to the acceptance of its evolution over millions of years. In each case, a system of beliefs was attached to a whole set of related ideas. It is to changes of this magnitude that Kuhn attaches the phrase "paradigm shift".

In the course of the 20th century, as Puerto Rican theologian Eunice Santana points out, there have been three great shifts in social consciousness: the anti-racism movement, the feminist movement and the ecological movement. By ending the formal structures of colonialism, the anti-racism movement changed the political geography of the world. By insisting that women have rights to personal autonomy, education, control of reproduction and equal participation in society, the feminist movement has had an impact on every society on earth. In hearing these messages, the churches and other receptive people are considering the signs of the times and responding to the Holy Spirit herself. So why, then, are racial minorities still oppressed, former colonies still impoverished, women still discriminated against and the environment still subject to assaults due to poverty and ill-controlled industrialization?

Because, Kuhn would say, moving from one paradigm to another takes a long time, and some individuals, institutions and nations take longer to move than others. For a while, a culture or group will be in the schizophrenic position of simultaneously operating out of two mutually incompatible paradigms, but without fully understanding this. Only after it is over is it possible to know that a paradigm shift has taken place: all one is aware of at the time is of living through a period of great moral, intellectual and spiritual confusion. There seems to be no going back, but no one is sure of the way forward either. Until it is over and the old beliefs have been broadly supplanted, the prophets of the new paradigm – the Galileos and the Darwins – are recognized, if at all, as trouble-makers, revolutionaries and dreamers.

One of my mother's favourite sayings was: "It's got to be gone through", which she used in times of trial such as moving house, our school exams and her own death from cancer. Participants in the Community Study, who were engaged in an uncomfortable journey, unable often to find a home in their own churches for the new insights it was bringing, chose for themselves the image of the "wilderness community..., not because it was a vote for withdrawal, rather because it offered a model of faithfulness."

Two decades later, I would like to suggest that the real "paradigm shift" has not so much been the changes around racism, feminism and ecology as the ontological reality of globalization, in the context of which all three movements are to be seen. Globalization is a shift in consciousness of a different order, since it underpins the whole structure of our understanding, our thinking about ourselves and our identities and cultures, and it governs the speed and urgency with which change itself can happen. Globalization is the reason why no racist incident, no abuse of power by men over women, no assault on the environment can ever again be seen as "a little local difficulty". Your story is my story; your story is our story. *For better or for worse.* And that has huge implications for the world church, for our thinking about religion and for our understanding of the nature of God. All of us are living through a time of great pain, great confusion and staggering opportunity. Like the incarnation and the crucifixion of the God who suffers, it's got to be gone through.

Patriarchy, theology and the Triune God

Mary Tanner suggests that one key ecclesiological question has come out of the Community Study and the Decade:

The central question was not about the inclusion women in the ordained ministry of the church, though that was a burning issue for many, nor was it about getting women into positions of authority in the church, though that too was an important issue. The central question to which all others were and remain related is the theological question of our understanding of the nature and being of God.

In this respect, the whole movement has benefited from the theological insights of the Orthodox churches. Participants in the Community Study spoke of their custom of displaying the Rublev icon of the Trinity at every meeting, stressing "the emerging emphasis in trinitarian theology on the personal and relational life of the Holy Trinity, on the receiving and giving, giving and receiving life of God, the utter mutual attentiveness of the persons to each other." For the new millennium, Pope John Paul II has commended the image of the Holy Trinity as the ultimate pattern, not just for the church but for the human community in general: the attentive, relational community grounded in mutuality and love, whose nature is to be in solidarity.

It is unfortunate, therefore, that so many women have problems with the Holy Trinity. While the figures in the Rublev icon are satisfactorily unisex, the Father, Son and Holy Spirit are normally represented in churches as an all-male trio, thus effectively excluding half the human race from what should be a life-giving blueprint for community. Theology cannot be rewritten in a day, but imagery is powerful, and women and men have often taken it upon themselves to make it more inclusive. The first and third persons of the Trinity – Father and Spirit – must in truth be genderless; yet, of all the churches' symbols of patriarchy, the *image* of God-as-male is the most heavily guarded. But often today the Holy Spirit is spoken of as "she". The Hebrew *ruah* is a feminine word, and many scholars believe that the original "type" for the New Testament Holy Spirit is the Old Testament personification of Sophia, Wisdom, represented as a female. The new community, born out of the unity of the Godhead, will be a non-starter if the language and symbolism in which it is experienced do not also reflect the relationality and inclusiveness of the Trinity.

Ecclesiological issues are raised both by the Community Study, with its emphasis on inclusiveness, and by the Decade, with its emphasis on the community of *women*. The Decade, says Aruna Gnanadason,

> calls for a new understanding of what it means to be the church. This is a deeper ecclesiological issue, not just one of justice and fair play... What women want is to build a new church, stripping it of its hierarchical and crippling institutionalism so that it could indeed be a movement of concerned and involved men and women, engaged in a ministry of healing and reconciliation.

What might be the hallmarks of such a church?

First, says Mary Tanner, the church is called to be a church of solidarity:

> Not "churches in solidarity with women", not even "women in solidarity with women". Rather, the fundamental nature and being of the church is that all – all men and women – are drawn into the life and love of God the Holy Trinity... What women have discovered together is not a truth about women but a profound truth about the graced life of belonging in the church – the holy, catholic and apostolic church – a church in unity. We are called to stand together with the poor, the marginalized, the victims of violence who are part of our own life in the church, to give voice to the voiceless, power to the powerless in our midst..., because that is the only kind of church that would mirror the sort of God in whom we believe.

The second ecclesiological challenge comes from the "world's agenda" – engaging violence and injustice on a global scale. As Aruna Gnanadason says, the church must be a *moral* community. "The connection between ecclesiology and ethics is fundamental... Without solidarity with the oppressed within its own life, without solidarity with the world's oppressed, the church cannot be truly one, holy, catholic or apostolic."

The third ecclesiological challenge is a challenge to the way the church is structured and power and authority are exercised. In reflecting on the Decade, feminist theologian Letty Russell writes that "everything feminists touch in a patriarchal society seems to turn to a question of authority – whose authority?" This is not just a question of representation, of women taking their place in the governing bodies of churches. It is a challenge to the patriarchal, male model of power that lies behind many church structures, which Letty Russell calls "the paradigm of domination". Her vision of "the church in the round", explored in her book of that title, is a helpful one.

The fourth ecclesiological challenge is related to the churches' agenda for mission. Traditionally, especially in the Protestant churches, Christian mission has been concerned with pro-active ministry or evangelization: the mission of "the church" to "the world". The experience of women has crucial messages in a world in which the *missio Dei* – God's mission – is increasingly understood as a holistic and inclusive invitation to become part of God's self-giving to the world. The challenge of *missio Dei* has to do with the nature of the self-giving God, in whom the "being" verbs (living alongside, being in solidarity, staying with, being reconciled with) are more important than the "doing" words (like serving, saving, building, winning).

To quote Mary Tanner again:

I have travelled a long way through two decades of challenge to the churches: the Community Study with its interlocking agenda, the vision of God, the understanding of women and men created in God's image, the inclusive life of the church that flows from that... And then the Decade with its challenges to inclusive life which flow from the experience of the solidarity women have experienced with women. All of these challenges are part of a single agenda, as our churches struggle to be an inclusive community. Inclusive community is not simply about getting more women into ordained ministry, or around tables where decisions are taken. It is the much, much more radical and fundamental agenda about theology, about what we believe about God, and about the nature of the church, about ecclesiology.

Always so angry? An eschatological perspective

In chronological terms, the history of organized Christian feminism has run more or less parallel with the history of the World Council of Churches. Although I am not old enough to remember those early days, my ecumenical formation and my formation as a feminist owe much to the men and women who pioneered both movements. Yet ecumenism and Christian feminism are both facing profound challenges today. Some of these come from the global nature of the ecumenical family: the pressure from the Orthodox and Roman Catholic churches to review the very structures of ecumenism, the dissatisfaction of African, Asian and Latin American churches with what they perceive to be the World Council's Western character and ethos. Others come from the community of young people, who want to open the windows and blow away ideological baggage which they perceive as irrelevant and life-denying.

The Decade has benefited immensely from the participation of young women. At the Harare Festival, they addressed a gathering of over a thousand. "Listen to us," they said. They are grateful to older women, their "mothers" in the movement, who have fought many fights and won important victories. They owe many of the opportunities they enjoy to the women who have gone before them. But the world has changed. In fighting for basic rights, the "mothers" have been forced into an operational style that is rooted in confrontation. They sometimes seem to believe they are part of a cosmic struggle in which men are the enemy.

There will still be a need to struggle, said the young women, but the adversarial spirituality which is the mark of the women's movement is no longer helpful. It focuses attention on the darkness, not the light. Individual men who are allies are alienated, and young men – many of whom have grown up in a more egalitarian age and do not see what the fuss is about – end up wondering what they have done to offend. It is time to move beyond a culture in which men can do no right, into a more inclusive vision of a community which will be better for all. The Decade is not a struggle between women and men, said a young woman from the Czech Republic, it is a struggle for women and men.

They spoke, too, of the danger of matriarchy within the movement. A matriarchal structure based on age and years of experience is the mirror image of patriarchy. "You are like our real mothers," said one young Nigerian woman. "You say to us, 'This is the way it must be done; this is the way we have learned to do it. You are young, you haven't learned to take life seriously. You don't understand.'" As a result, a new orthodoxy is born, a new fundamentalism, and the voice of the future is silenced.

The young women commented on the challenge to women who do make it into positions of authority. "Women can be more authoritarian and hierarchical than men," observes Priyanka Mendis from Sri Lanka. "They think it is wrong to have fun. They do not encourage other women. There is an assumption that women are oppressed. What we need is role models of women who have stopped being oppressed."

"I feel I was born into this hierarchy of suffering," said a young woman from the United States. "If I am not suffering myself, then I think I cannot be doing it right. But if I am going to suffer, I want it to be because of my own agenda, and not my mother's."

"Trust us," said the young women.

For me, the most moving thing was the attention with which the young women's voices were heard and the seriousness with which they were taken. Ten years ago, said several women, young women could not have spoken like that, with such a combination of challenge and love, and expected to be heard. The Decade has done something if it has taught us to listen to our daughters. In my mind, I have labelled this section "eschatology": not because it is about death, but because the vision of the young women does seem to me to reach beyond diversity to community, beyond brokenness to healing, beyond confrontation to reconciliation. This is not

Good News for the Poor?

(Luke 4:16-20)

Mary is happy. It is the eve of the sabbath, and after months of travelling, her son is at home. He says he has been fasting in the desert for six weeks. His face is haggard, his bones protrude, his hair is long. She watches him now, devouring the flat breadcakes she has just cooked for him. If only he would stay for a while, so that she could look after him, get some flesh on his bones. Outside, Mary can hear the little ones playing, Joseph's grandchildren and, for all practical purposes, hers.[1] Just now, however, she is trying to enjoy the eve-of-sabbath calm, and the rare treat of having her beloved son beside her.

She is restless, though, and anxious. Tonight Jesus will be reading in the synagogue. She has prayed for this appearance to go well, but with him you just never know what to expect. Since he came home he has been full of a kind of restless fire. If only he could be more *normal.* Mary sighs. Either people love him or they hate him. She sometimes thinks he *enjoys* rubbing them up the wrong way. The past flashes before her: the miracle of the child in her womb, the incredible events that followed his birth, the time they spent as refugees in Egypt. Her wild outburst to her old dear old cousin, with child herself, when she first knew she was pregnant. *My soul magnifies the Lord...* Again and again, she has had to accept his uniqueness, the fact that he belongs, in some mysterious way, to God and not to her. *Never* to her. *You would think I would be used to it by now,* she reflects. She thinks about the strange intimacy of his relationship with God: *Abba,* he says when he talks to God. *Daddy.*

In the synagogue, Mary squats down at the back with the other women, the girls and the smaller boys, while Jesus and the brothers march to the front. Word has reached Nazareth of the carpenter's son who is making a name for himself as a healer, and the place is packed. From where she is she can see little. But the candles are lit, the familiar ritual unfolds, the scrolls are produced, and she realizes that her son has stood up to read.

Tonight it is the much-loved passage from Isaiah, in which the prophet proclaims a year of Jubilee for the poor. "The Spirit of the Lord is upon me...," the beautiful words ring out. *It will be all right,* thinks Mary, relaxing. Jesus reads on. "He has anointed me to bring good news to the poor. He has sent me to proclaim release to the captives and recovery of sight to the blind, to let the oppressed go free, to proclaim the year of the Lord's favour." She knows it by heart. He sits down, and there is an expectant pause. The text speaks strongly to a community whose major income is from servicing rich people in the nearby Gentile city, and they are waiting for him to say more. "Today," he says, not getting up, "today this prophecy has been fulfilled in your presence."

There is a hush, and then a great cheer goes up. Excited voices are raised. "Free us from oppression, Jesus!" "An end to poverty!" "Bring in the year of Jubilee!" In front of her a woman is saying, "The carpenter's son has turned out well!" Another calls, "Is that your boy, Mary?"

Through the throng, she sees him rise to his feet again. Her heart sinks. He has *that look* on his face. "No doubt you are going to say to me, 'Do here in your home town the things you did in Capernaum,'" says Jesus. "But no prophet is ever accepted in the prophet's hometown. The truth is that there were many widows in Israel in the time of Elijah, when the heaven was shut up for three years and six months, and there was a severe famine over the land; yet Elijah was sent to none of these but to a widow at Zarephath in Sidon..." In the sudden hubbub, Mary is having difficulty hearing: "... was sent to a foreigner... Elisha... leprosy... but only Naaman the Syrian was cleansed, and he was an outcast and an oppressor." And her son sits down.

There is a stunned silence. The people of Nazareth are poor, but they are a close-knit community, proud of their religion, proud to be God's own people. Foreigners may be richer or more powerful, but they, as the children of Israel, are the chosen ones. Now here is this local lad, Joseph's son, using their own scriptures to say that his good news is not for them, but for those whom they reject and despise. *How could you, Jesus?,* she whispers. In this synagogue, what he has said is heresy, and they will not forgive.

There is a rumble, then a great shout of fury, and the men are on their feet, surging towards him. "Out with him!", shouts one voice. "Throw him over the cliff!", screams another. Helplessly, Mary watches him disappear behind the pack. Rooted to the spot, clutching a terrified child who has been squatting near her, she sees them hustle him out of the building and into the dusk.

She never works out quite what happens next. As she is hurrying up the hill after the baying mob, she meets groups of men trickling back towards the synagogue. It is almost dark when she arrives, out of breath, at the cliff-edge – too dark to see his broken body lying there below. "What happened?", she asks hesitantly. But they push her aside and turn back to one another, loud and angry.

Uncertainly, Mary turns back the way she has come. What next? She looks back ironically at her contentment a few hours earlier. Will it always be like this? Will she never learn? Miserably she trails back home.

The house is dark, silent and empty, the carefully prepared sabbath meal unlikely now to be eaten.[2] In the lamplight she can see his little bundle of possessions lying in the corner. It occurs to her that he may never be able to return here after today, that if she wants to be near him and look after him, she will have to leave home and follow him. Thank God Joseph did not live to see this day! *Why do you do it, Jesus?*, asks her heart. *Can't you ever make it easy for yourself?*

Into her mind comes a picture: the solemn boy sitting in the temple in Jerusalem, locked in debate with the teachers; her frantic worry; Joseph's furious anger. Then the wide, serious eyes, the piping child's voice: "Don't you know that I must be about my Father's business?" What pain this child has brought her! *What pain is still to come.*

Footsteps are hurrying up the street. Her eldest stepson James pushes into the lamplit room. "It's OK," he says. "We got him away. And I've come for his things. But he may not be so lucky next time. *Why does he do it?*"

In her heart Mary knows exactly why he does it. "He thinks they are too smug and too comfortable," she says forlornly. "He thinks God is for everybody, and that justice means putting outsiders *first*, not last. He wants to break down walls so that the outsiders can come in. But they feel safe only when they are building walls to keep the outsiders out. Which means they are always going to hate him."

And they will get him in the end, she is about to add, but James has already gone. There in the little house in Nazareth, Mary buries her head in her arms and weeps. Not for the first time she has the sensation of entering unknown territory. *I don't understand,* she wails, *I just don't understand.* She feels drained and empty. *Help!,* she sobs.

The memory of *that day* comes into her mind, and she puts a hand on her womb. How strong she was then; what power she was given. And all for this? From across the years, the words she has so often pondered ring in her ears: *Fear not, Mary, for you have found favour with God.* The same mixture of awe and astonishment sweeps over her, and she recalls her own words: *All generations shall call me blessed.*

"I had no idea," she says aloud. "I was so innocent, then." Yet what can she do? Her love for this strange child of hers is the most important thing in her life, always has been, always will be.

Be it unto me according to thy word, says her heart. She will do what has to be done.

NOTES

[1] Many mainstream New Testament scholars believe that Joseph was an elderly widower when Mary married him, and that "Jesus' brothers" were the sons of Joseph by a previous marriage.
[2] The *shabat* meal was eaten on the evening before the sabbath.

3. At the Edge of the Cliff

The antidote to Africa's economic dilemma:
Go to the villages,
behind mountains, hills and valleys
Who do you see? Woman!

Jeaniville Wase, Cameroon

"What did you come to Africa to see?", asked Musimbi Kanyoro. "A people stricken with disease and disaster? You can see all that on CNN. Internationally, when you watch television you have to wait for something really horrible to happen before you know Africa exists. What did *you* come to Africa to see?"

I have found this question difficult for two reasons. The first is that although people generalize about Africa all the time, Africa is so big, so diverse, so pluralistic, and so many things to so many people that there will always be someone for whom what you say is not the way it is. The second is that while Africa is uniquely Africa, many of its current political and economic problems are the same as those faced by the formerly-colonized countries of Asia and Latin America.

In response to the first problem, I have tried to set out responses to Africa in such a way as to honour diversity while accepting the need, shared by Africans and non-Africans alike, to say at least *something* that might be described as generally true. As for economics and debt, I have left this section to the end and tried to relate it to the broad situation of crisis that exists in the two-thirds world generally. Perhaps this was not the best-possible solution, and I apologize to Asian and Latin American women who think these issues should have had a chapter to themselves.

What did I go to Africa to see? What did I see when I got there?

There is the Africa of CNN, whose travel programmes on African wildlife, with their stunningly beautiful scenery, alternate with the stories of suffering and disaster and war on its news programmes. There is the Africa its politicians want you to see, and the day-to-day Africa its people experience. There is the symbolic Africa: Africa and what it means to its own African peoples, which is not the same meaning Africa has for the rest of the world. There is Africa "the Dark Continent", and there is Africa where the sun shines. There is the Africa which carries on its body the scars and open wounds of its political and economic relationship with North America and Europe – which are the same as many of the scars on the bodies of Asian and Latin American nations. There is the Africa which is one people, and the Africa which is many peoples and many nations. There is the Africa which forgives, and the Africa which is furiously angry. There is the instinctive hospitality of Africans, and the painful awareness that such sharing may cause real hardship.

There was the Africa *we* saw, and the Africa I personally encountered. There is the Africa of women and the Africa of men.

Having come expecting to see Africa, we saw many Africas; and, reflected in them, we saw the world. So, having made it clear that Musimbi Kanyoro's question is impossible to answer, let me try to do so.

First, *we*. We encountered people who were unstintingly warm and generous. We took to ourselves the exuberant, rhythmic music of Africa, the irresistible magnetism of the dancing and the wonderful, instinctive harmonies of the singing. We were soothed or excited by the spare beauty of the land, the red earth, the magic sunsets.

What especially struck those of us who are not African were the contrasts we saw. We encountered celebration and despair, privilege and poverty, great self-sacrifice and extreme violence. We found cruelty and generosity, corruption and transparent honesty, oppression and a passionate belief in the liberated spirit. We found love, and we found rage. We were blinded by the hot sun, soaked in downpours.

In Zimbabwe itself we also found acute anxiety about the effects of debt, the collapsing Zimbabwe dollar and the teetering health and education services. There was general fury about the involvement of Zimbabwean troops in the war in Congo, and the millions of dollars it is costing the economy. There was an erosion of confidence in government, combined with tales of corruption, and fear that the results of land redistribution (or the delay of land distribution) will be more inequitable than the present situation. There was anger and despair about massive price rises. We found confused helplessness about the steady advance of HIV infection in this country which is said to have the highest percentage of new cases of any country in the world. In the crowded streets of Harare, merchants and shoppers were preparing for Christmas. Tourists were everywhere, and the shops were full of things to buy; but there was also an almost tangible unease, as a proud, hopeful and well-organized country began to wonder whether it might be looking into the abyss.

As for me personally, I was going back to the continent which is the scene of my earliest memories, where I spent part of my childhood, where I went to primary school and to which I always return with a sense of homecoming. I was returning to a continent where my ancestors ventured, believing in a now-discredited dream; where my parents spent many years; and where many of my most deeply formative experiences took place. As an Englishwoman and a member of my own family, I am acutely conscious of the moral ambiguity of my relationship with Africa, and also of my love for that huge, mysterious continent which I personally have never found to be "dark".

So what did I see?

- I saw the mighty power of the "smoke that thunders", internationally known (after a former queen of my own country) as Victoria Falls.
- I saw women dancing and singing of hope, in the midst of civil war.
- I saw a school with no roof, no desks and no chairs.
- I saw a dispensary with few medicines and no rubber gloves.
- I saw a widowed mother of seven, dying of AIDS, with no drugs to contain the sickness or pain.
- I heard an account of a bomb attack in Southern Sudan. "The animals provided us with an advance warning facil-

ity. Dogs hastened to the bunkers. A pet monkey joined them. Hens and chickens took off in hurried flight to the shade beneath the nearest bushes. Birds stopped singing. A sudden stillness gripped all. We quickly followed those dogs and the monkey to the bunkers. Animals and humans shared a paralyzing fear."

- I heard a Sudanese woman say, "We are bleeding to death. Can you tell me, has the world forgotten about us?"
- I heard a Congolese woman say, "Please ask anyone interfering in another country to go back to their own."
- I heard a South African say, "Corruption is theft from the poor."
- I heard a woman from Sierra Leone say, "My country is full of guns. Africa is full of guns. But Africa does not manufacture guns. So where are they all coming from?"
- I saw the scars from machete gashes on the face, head and neck of a Rwandan woman, who said, "I lost all my children in the genocide."
- I met a Ghanaian teacher who spoke of the progress she saw being made in the schools.
- I met African women who furiously rejected victim status, and others who insisted on retaining it.
- I met an Englishwoman who had visited a refugee camp in Khartoum on her way southwards. She spoke of women who brewed illicit alcohol because there was nothing to live on. They were arrested and flogged, and now 1300 women are living, with their children, in a prison meant for 400. They speak of living in hope, because there is nothing else to do.
- I heard an African proverb quoted by a Kenyan woman: "I pointed out the moon to you, but all you saw was my finger."
- I saw a million stars.
- I met a Zimbabwean woman who is on the executive committee of the Zimbabwe Council of Churches. She said, "Our dear fathers were not aware that they were oppressing us. But now we have talked a lot, and now they are aware!"

What Africans say

When Africans are allowed to tell their own story, it may be the story of Mama Afrika, the cradle of the human race, the fountain of civilization, robbed of its soul by colonization. It may be the earth which the ancestors will ultimately call back to its ancient values. It may be the place where the holy family sought refuge from Herod's murderous thugs. Here, faith in the Creator God is ingrained, and so is an awareness of the force of evil.

Barney Pityana rejects both the glorification of Africa's past and the gloom and doom of those who would like to see Africa as a victim. Either approach, he says, encourages Africans to believe that everyone but themselves is to blame for the fate of Africa, thus preventing them from taking responsibility for their politics, their economy and their culture. He speaks of three challenges facing Africans: the eradication of poverty; the establishment of democracy, human rights and good systems of governance; and the setting of standards for a moral universe. Africa is in crisis, yes: but African people journey in faith. Africa, he says, is the footprint of the incarnate God, a pilgrim people, accompanied on the road by their ancestors, always journeying, worshipping God because it is their nature as Africans to do so.

E.B. Idowu suggests that what powerful nations expect of Africa is the very same thing that most societies expect of women. This view is reinforced by Ali Mazrui, who describes Africa as "the female continent – passive, patient and penetrable". Ghanaian theologian Mercy Amba Oduyoye condemns the use of such imagery. Women resent these stereotypes, she says, "so Africa must refuse this female typology". Mama Afrika is a powerful symbol, but it is also a dangerous one:

> Where she behaves herself according to prescription and accepts an inferior position, the benevolence which her "poverty" demands is assured; and for this she shows herself deeply and humbly grateful. If for some reason she takes it into her head to be assertive and claim a footing of equality, then she brings upon herself a frown; she is called names; she is perse-

cuted openly or by indirect means; she is helped to be divided against herself.

Mercy Oduyoye describes the 20th century as "Africa's Christian century". She says she is filled "with fear and trembling" by the rapid growth in the number of Christians in Africa: from some 10 million Christians to an estimated 329 million in the course of the 20th century. What worries her most is that the church has grown evangelically without developing a corresponding theological, liturgical and economic maturity. "There are many more churches, many more expatriate missionaries, many more charismatic movements and many more people who confess Christ their personal Saviour. There are many who leave it to The Christ to deal with their enemy, The Devil."

As a result, she says, instead of accepting the challenge of the incarnation, and getting on with the job of developing culturally appropriate models of worship and of action in society, many African churches continue to market an expatriate religion which provides a refuge from the real challenges of being African today. To address this situation, the Circle of Concerned African Women Theologians was formed.

"Talitha Qumi"

The Circle of Concerned African Women Theologians was the brainchild of Mercy Oduyoye and Rosemary Edet, a Nigerian religious. Founded in 1989, the Circle today numbers over 350 affiliated members from across the continent, most of them black Christian theologians working in education, universities, seminaries, teacher training colleges, nongovernmental organizations, international para-church organizations, and as church ministers, health workers and teachers.

The network is designed to encourage the publication of African women's perspectives on issues of contemporary concern, such as marriage regulations, domestic violence, widowhood rites, international inequalities and social con-

structions of motherhood. It also seeks to promote the place
of women in traditional religion, and in mission and independent churches. Other work addresses cultural and historical issues important to women. In *Women, Presbyterianism
and Patriarchy,* Malawian Presbyterian Isabel Phiri argues
that women's power was well-established in the traditional
matrilineal religion of the Chewa people of central Malawi.
But the churches founded by Christian missionaries from
Europe and North America were hostile to matrilineality, justifying male privilege by reference to Genesis 2:7-24, the
pastoral epistles and the Pauline advocacy of male headship
(Eph. 5:21-24). Not much has changed. When Isabel Phiri
published her study, she was hounded and victimized, and
her family was threatened. Eventually she had to leave her
job.

To bring about ecclesiological change, activism is useful
up to a certain point. Many men in the churches are sympa-
thetic to the cause of women, and recognize it as a human
rights issue. Ultimately, however, it is doomed to failure
unless it is backed up by theological research and argument.
It is from the scriptures that the churches claim justification
for patriarchy; and they are not going to be dislodged from
this base simply by "women making a nuisance of themselves". The attention of the Circle has thus turned to the
study of biblical hermeneutics, anthropology and mission
history; and work is being done on studying alternative and
empowering texts from the perspective of African women.
The Circle's first publication was entitled *Talitha Qumi*,
literally "Little girl, arise": the words Jesus addressed to
Jairus's twelve-year-old daughter (Mark 5:41).

Women who received their Christian formation from mission churches in colonized countries sometimes distrust the
Bible, feeling that it is an instrument of colonization and
male domination. The Circle however has taken the view that
the Bible is a liberating text for African women because of
the significant parallels between the contexts of biblical
women and African women today. If biblical women suffered from an oppressive cultural status quo, so do African

women today. Among the common issues faced are single parenthood, polygamy, surrogacy, widowhood, prostitution and the low economic and legal status of women.

The fact that this is an *African* women's initiative is of fundamental importance for the rest of the world. The Circle is a continent-wide network, carving out a counter-tradition within the dominant traditions of "male-stream" theology. In so doing, it is taking a prophetic stance, speaking of freedom, well-being and hope in the midst of economic injustice and disaster. In this, it has much in common with the work of many US and Asian feminist theologians. For example, African-American "womanist" theology is deeply aware of its roots in the history of an oppressed people. In contrast to the Circle, it speaks less of liberation than of women's capacity for survival and their ability to introduce an element of humanity into the most brutalized context.

African women often remark on the adversarial quality of Western feminism. This means, a Ugandan friend told me, that it will never make headway in African society. In Africa, she said, the relationship between women and men lies at the very heart of the culture, and shifts in the balance of power are only possible with agreement of both, and of the community or institution itself.

The Circle has made a conscious decision against bringing the "war of the sexes" into the churches of Africa. Mercy Oduyoye repeatedly emphasizes the need for co-operation with African men, not antagonism. The indebtedness of Africa and its civil dislocation require what she calls a "two-winged" theology, in which women and men together work together to support life and fight against death.

> But Lord, we are all passers-by
> You created us male and female
> for a rich and more fulfilled life.
> The world would not be the same
> with one sex to accomplish your plan.
> No one remains the same for ever:
> We come and go,
> We shine and fade away,

We are born to die,
Our home is in you.

Grace Eneme, Cameroon

The female face of poverty

The data are all too familiar: the increasing gap between rich and poor, the erosion of health, education and welfare services for poor people worldwide, the huge pressures being placed on national budgets by the repayment of debts incurred by other governments in other days, the Structural Adjustment Policies imposed by international financial institutions in the hope of putting economies back in order. In the ten years of the Decade, the share of global income going to the poorest 20 percent of the world's people has dropped from 2.3 percent to 1.4 percent.

It has also become clearer in recent years that while poverty affects men as well as women, the major burden is carried by women. Biasima Lala spoke of this at a plenary session on women in Harare:

> In the countries of Europe and North America, most working women are in the lowest-paid job categories. They are the most affected by the reduction of social spending and by job cutbacks, losing not only their salaries but also their retirement pensions. Thus there is an ever-increasing gap between rich and poor, but especially between the economic situation of men and women.
>
> In the developing countries, women are subjected to a double martyrdom by the economic crisis: first as poor women without education, second as wives of chronically unemployed and unpaid workers who sometimes have to move away from home in pursuit of usually hypothetical employment. The full weight of the survival of home and family then falls on women's shoulders, often to the detriment of their health.

Living Letters, the report of the mid-Decade visits, offers a wealth of information about the economic position of women. In rural areas, with agricultural prices falling, men may depart to work in the cities, leaving their families behind them: an option which women rarely have (Argentina, Mexico, Pakistan, Indonesia). In addition, family illness or the care of a dependent relative is more likely to prevent women from doing paid work. In industrialized societies, women are particularly vulnerable to exploitation. "The manufacturing industries in the free trade zones employ mostly young women, who are exposed to discrimination, social insecurity and violence, if not outright discrimination" (Malaysia). In Eastern Europe, the growth in capitalism has led to great wealth for some, unemployment and acute poverty for others. "Some women are so desperate that they have themselves sterilized to increase their chances of getting jobs" (former German Democratic Republic).

The sex industry is booming. From Thailand, the Philippines, South Africa, Romania, Mexico and many other places come tales of increased trafficking in young girls (and also, incidentally, boys). The girls are often born into poor families who are only too willing to believe that they are doing their best for their daughter by sending her off to train as a "waitress" or a "maid". The evidence of poverty-related prostitution comes from all parts of the world. Of particular concern are the stories of AIDS widows, rejected by families and having to fend for themselves on the streets. Or as a woman from Lesotho said, "The men often go to South Africa to work in the mines. Often the money does not come in as expected, and women are left to find other ways of feeding and educating their kids."

The vulnerability of women starts in the womb. In some cultures, the birth of daughters may be treated as an occasion for commiseration not congratulation, spelling economic catastrophe for poor families. The dowry system in India and the one-child family policy in China place pressure on couples to produce boys, and technology now makes it possible to abort unwanted girl children before they are born. Where they do survive to birth, girl children are less likely to be educated, taken to the doctor, treated when they become ill.

In recent years, the global market and the international financial institutions have operated in such a way as to remove clear choices from even those national governments genuinely committed to relieving poverty. The phrase "global village, global pillage" sums it up all too well. Privatization and debt-restructuring have combined to produce cuts in services to poor people, and the consequent deterioration in the health of women and children and the coping capacity of many families has been well documented in all regions. Where you live seems to be increasingly irrelevant. It used to be said that the rest of the world catches a cold if the United States of America sneezes. Today, if South Korea or Brazil sneezes, Washington and Brussels start reaching for the Kleenex. Only you cannot win, because you will then find that Kleenex is marketed by a US-based international conglomerate of companies.

In many parts of the world, churches which have faced up to this situation are doing noble work to address it. From Peru and Chile come stories of church involvement with slum populations and indigenous people. Pentecostal communities were particularly mentioned as giving dignity to women who learn to participate in prayer and witness. In South India, all the churches have programmes to improve the economic situation of women, seeing these as improving the health and education of families and decreasing the likelihood of violence against women. Churches in Kenya have a network of economic projects operated by women, including agriculture and food production programmes, small business ventures, craft co-operatives and credit loan schemes, often rooted in the lives of the local congregations.

Many churches are engaged, thoughtfully and professionally, in their traditional Christian calling to respond to the ills of society and minister to those in need. Money is raised to support these activities, and congregations are often personally involved in their implementation. The feminization of poverty is seen as a justice issue, and one which Christian compassion is bound to acknowledge. Yet the mid-Decade teams, focusing on economic issues, found little evidence of parallel change within the churches themselves. While the arguments for change in society seem to have been accepted,

the ecclesiological implications of these arguments have yet
to be faced.

Women love the church, they work for it, many parishes
would fall apart without their commitment, and they are
rarely paid for what they do. But listen to some of the findings recorded in *Living Letters:* From Cameroon, "Pastors
use the money we raised without informing us where and
how it goes." From Canada, "Finance and property seem to
be the province of men in many congregations, and women
are excluded from financial decision-making." From South
Korea, "We were told that the church does not pay pensions
for the hundreds of women evangelists actively engaged in
grassroots ministry." From Cameroon, again: "Despite a
massive government awareness campaign on the situation of
widows – which the churches themselves initiated – the latter have not followed through with appropriate measures.
When widows are forced into prostitution or must sell illegal
drugs or alcohol, the churches often denounce the morality of
such activities but rarely concern themselves with the reasons." Mid-Decade teams were horrified to realize that
women in some Christian communities are regarded as
replaceable property, that wives and daughters are considered of less value than the domestic animals.

"The major issue here is poverty," said a Zambian pastor.
"Whether to use 'he' or 'she' is a petty thing. What matters is
whether she or he has anything in their stomach." It is a com-
pelling argument. But it is at best fantasy and at worst
hypocrisy to claim that churches can address issues of economic injustice without also addressing their attitudes to
women.

Good news for the poor?

The story told in Luke 4:16-30 – the Window which precedes this chapter – has been a key text for the ecumenical
movement, and it was the gospel reading for the opening
worship at the WCC's assembly in Harare. Its announcement
of "the year of the Lord's favour" speaks of the theme of
Jubilee, the remission of debt and the restoration of a just

order. For the following insights, I am indebted to the wonderful Bible study group in which I took part in Harare, and to Brian Davies of the Catholic Fund for Overseas Development (CAFOD) in the United Kingdom.

The scroll from which Jesus reads to the people of his own village is a popular one: Isaiah's words about the one who is anointed to bring good news to the poor, release to the captives, sight to the blind and freedom to the oppressed, and a year of jubilee. Waiting expectantly for what will come next, they are delighted when he says, "Today this prophecy is fulfilled in your sight" though it is not clear what they understand his meaning to be. Yet ten verses – and maybe ten minutes – later they are baying for his blood and want to throw him over a cliff.

What has happened in these ten verses? The people of Nazareth were poor. Since most of them probably worked in the nearby Gentile city of Sepphoris, they saw economic change as related to their own poverty and the relative wealth of others. Still, as members of the synagogue, they were respectable and God-fearing, part of the religious establishment of the town.

Then Jesus reminded them of two familiar stories from the book of Kings. Elijah, he says, could have used the power God gave him to help any one of Israel's many widows; instead, he chose to help a foreigner, a widow of Sidon, a region devoted to the worship of Baal. And when his successor Elisha healed a man with leprosy, it was not one of the many lepers in Israel but Naaman the Syrian. In neither case did salvation have strings attached. The news of salvation, says Jesus, is not for the insiders in the synagogue at Nazareth. It is for the outcast, the foreigner. This gospel "subtext" to the message of Jubilee, which provides the theological roots for the church's call to the remission of debt, seems to be deeply threatening in ways that go far beyond the imaginings of the comfortable.

It would have been much easier if Jesus had stopped after the announcement that the prophecy of jubilee was fulfilled in the here and now. No doubt Mary, still in the process of dis-

Let the Children Be Fed First?

(Mark 7:24-30; Matthew 15:21-28)

When the screaming started, it was still dark. Since then, the moments of silence have been the hush of temporary exhaustion only. Now, in the midday heat, the darkness of the little house is torn again by shrieks, by head-banging and by the convulsive jerking which Kyria has come to dread. The child's eyes are unseeing, the bruised face smeared with foam.

Rebecca is her youngest child, her only girl baby to survive infancy, and Kyria loves her with a painful passion. Never strong, she is left weaker by every seizure. Only her mother's single-minded attention has kept her alive this long. Eventually, the screaming will stop, and it will be forever...

Today, torn between love and near-violent desperation, Kyria catches herself hoping that the end, if it must come, will be soon. Because if this goes on, they will starve to death anyway. She cannot leave the child on her own while she is like this, or she will kill herself. So Kyria cannot go to the fields, she will not earn money, and the boys will come home and find there is nothing for supper. Again.

She is so alone. With her quick tongue and her sharp, domineering intelligence, she knows that the neighbours find her difficult to like. In a society where acceptance depends on having a man, a woman on her own should be grateful to be spoken to at all. Who knows why her husband left? She can see it in their eyes. But she is a competent woman, and so long as she and the children are well, she manages.

Recently the landlord, who also owns the fields in which she works, has been making threatening noises about her repeated absences. Does he think she is staying away on purpose? Already he keeps back one-third of what she earns each week to pay interest on the money she has borrowed from him over the years. Every night she lies in the dark, sweating with anxiety about these debts and wondering whether the time has come to do what so many others have done. Living on the main road, she can, if all else fails, sell her body to one of the travellers who pass her door. But if she had anything else left, she would give it to the person who would make her daughter whole.

Outside, there is commotion. Something is happening. Another political demonstration? Somebody selling something? She peers out of the door. Accustomed to the darkness of her own house, dazzled by the sun, she can see nothing. "It's the healer from Galilee!", shouts someone. She has heard of this Israelite healer – everyone has. He must be one of that little group of men padding swiftly down the dusty road, heads bowed, in the midst of the excited crowd of local people.

On an impulse she hurtles from her doorway, head uncovered, clutching her skirts and half-blinded by the light. "Have mercy on me, Lord," she shouts. "My daughter is sick." The crowd freezes. This mad-looking woman has done the unthinkable: she has spoken out aggressively in the company of these men, and now here she is, chasing after them. The Galileans falter. Most look away, embarrassed. But one of them keeps walking, locked in his private world, as if she has not spoken at all.

Kyria knows this must be the one. Frantically, she stumbles after him. "Son of David,"[1] she calls, "My daughter is tormented by a demon." The quiet one walks on, oblivious.

"She keeps on bothering us, Master" says one of his friends. "Tell her to shut up and get lost!"

Jesus stops. He sees her eyes, red with tears and exhaustion, blinded by sunlight. He takes in her dishevelled appearance. A Gentile, of course.[2] "You must know that I was sent only for the lost sheep of the house of Israel," he says gently.

And of course Kyria does know this. The Israelites have always been the top dogs, arrogantly confident that their God is their exclusive property. All the rest – Samaritans, Canaanites, Egyptians, Romans and so on – are unclean, untouchable, excluded by birth from this magic circle. She has grown up taking all this for granted. She is also a woman, and should never have spoken out like that in the first place. Her wild chase after this unknown healer was insane. All this she knows. If only she could go back and start the conversation again.... But she thinks

60

of Rebecca, and falls on her knees before him, she who kneels to no one. She has nothing left to lose. "Help me, Master," she begs.

"I cannot," answers the quiet man. "It is not fair to let the dogs have the food intended for the children of the house."

She feels as if he has hit her. She was wrong about him. The kind eyes have deceived her. But then to him, of course, she *is* less than human. No point in arguing, then. Anyway, what does it matter what he thinks of her? At this moment, all she cares about is Rebecca. *Yes, but...*, says her head. *You may think I am mad*, says her heart, *but I don't care what you think of me. Please, Lord, heal my darling child*. And from nowhere, it seems, the words come. "Yes, Master," she says aloud, getting clumsily to her feet so that she can look him in the face. "Yes. But even the dogs under the table are allowed to finish the children's crumbs."

The crowd falls silent. Nobody has ever heard a woman answering back like that, as if she were an equal. What will happen now? But Kyria holds her ground. There is a long pause, so long that she begins to wonder if the healer has heard her. He has been visibly startled by her response. Now he is looking at her thoughtfully, his keen eyes troubled. What is he thinking? "You have great faith,"[3] he says at last, almost dismissively. "Go back to your daughter: the demon has left her." He turns back to his friends, the little party sets off again, and this time she does not try to stop them.

The dark house, when she re-enters it, is quiet. Thumb in mouth, Rebecca is asleep. Kyria's legs are shaking. Her throat aches with unshed tears. As the first of them fall, the black lashes flicker on the sweet, fragile face. Her daughter wakes. "Don't cry, *Amma*," she murmurs. "I'll be fine now."

NOTES

[1] She addresses Jesus as a Jew – she is aware of the racial problem.
[2] Matthew refers to her as a Canaanite woman; Mark emphasizes that she was a Gentile, possibly seeing her as the prototype of Gentile women who believe.
[3] Matthew says it is the woman's faith which convinces Jesus. For Mark, it is her arguments.

4. Which Women?

They act as if my people's wounds were only scratches.
"All is well," they say, when all is not well.

Jeremiah 6:14

The root of oppression is loss of memory

The fight against racism became a priority for the World Council of Churches in the early 1960s; and a programme on Women Under Racism became part of the Programme to Combat Racism. Since that time, discrimination on grounds of race has become illegal in many countries, as more and more nations are becoming patchworks of different racial and ethnic groups. Yet economic and professional racism, exploitation of racial minorities and cultural exclusion on grounds of race seem as prevalent as they ever were. As the 1983 Vancouver assembly was told, "Racism, sexism, class domination, denial of people's rights, caste oppression are all woven together like a spider's web... They are at the root of many injustices which cause much suffering and death."

Speaking to the WCC assembly in Harare, Mukami McCrum from Scotland put it bluntly. In every part of the world, racial minorities, migrant women and indigenous women have been failed by both the church and the women's movement. The "stone of racism" has barely been dislodged, let alone rolled away. "What Decade?", ask indigenous women. And more to the point, "Which women?"

Olivia Juarez comes from Mexico, colonized by the Spanish in the 15th century. Without reclaiming history and rewriting it from the viewpoint of the powerless, she says, it is impossible to understand the situation of indigenous women. When the Spanish arrived, they encountered people from an ancient and honourable culture. These men and women lived differently, looked different and spoke no language the Spanish had ever heard. To the newcomers from Europe, they seemed a different species, but strong and capable and therefore ideally fitted to slavery. It was said that they felt no pain, so it became permissible to mark or brand a slave as a sign of ownership. It was also believed that they had no moral sense, so fierce punishments were needed to make them behave in a "civilized" – that is, European – way.

To the Spanish, the indigenous people of Mexico gave their work, and the mineral and agricultural wealth of their country. What the Spanish brought them was violence. Many Spanish men had come to the American continent without their womenfolk. Female slaves were therefore particularly vulnerable. Seduced, battered and raped, many gave birth to half-caste children. To their masters, they were still slaves; now they became objects of scorn within their own communities, both as sexually abused women and as mothers of foreigners.

Today, many indigenous women live in the cities. Here they are still exploited. As domestic servants, they work long hours. Many have experienced rape or attempted rape by bosses and their sons. The assumption is that they offered themselves voluntarily, and they are subject to instant dismissal if the incident is discovered. Because rural people may speak no other language than their own, they are thought of as animals and treated in schools as idiots. Some work as street vendors, but robbery is frequent, and the police do not take attacks on so-called Indians as seriously as if they were "white". Everywhere, women suffer double discrimination, on grounds of race first, and then as women. Many have joined the rebel movements, believing that whatever the risk, it is better to struggle for a more dignified life than to suffer in hopelessness.

As an indigenous woman, says Olivia Juarez, the most important thing for her has been to reclaim her own history. Not that this changes the way she is treated, but it does help her to understand and deal with cultural, academic and professional exclusion she meets, the violence with which the academic establishment rejects and silences the insights of indigenous people in general and indigenous women in particular.

The report of the mid-Decade visits gives examples of the history of indigenous, colonialized and minority peoples being driven underground by the story of the colonialist power or majority group. Some members of these colonialist "master-races" may be committed to developing non-racist attitudes and may even have a limited understanding of their own sub-conscious racism; but despite their good will they find it difficult to acknowledge its influence on structures and on culture. The mid-Decade teams found much evidence of this.

"I only know how to oppress," confessed a white South African woman. "That was all I was taught. We were taught that we were superior, and we did not speak or mix with non-whites. For many whites, it has been upsetting to hear black people say, 'We have rights too.'" She was aware of her upbringing but not of how this same dynamic was being played out in the meeting in which she made this acknowledgment. There are those who are used to having power over others and to being in control, and there are those who stay silent unless deliberate efforts are made to give them space to contribute.

Colonialism is not the only thing that produces discrimination against ethnic groups. In her best-selling novel *God of Small Things,* Indian Christian Arundathi Roy paints a powerful picture of the caste system in her native Kerala. In India, Dalit communities fall outside the caste system. Known formerly as "untouchables", they lived under a kind of apartheid, legally permitted to do only the dirtiest and most unpleasant jobs. Today they are protected by law; nevertheless, as one Dalit woman told the mid-Decade team, "Dalit women are the oppressed of the oppressed. They are so often ill-treated that violence is almost the name of their lives. If we are to look for Christ's scars, we shall find them on the body of Dalit women."

In many parts of the world, churches have stood with people of colour in their struggles for political and economic justice. Thoko Mpulwana learned about activism in the church from her parents: her father was a pastor in Kwazulu Natal, her mother was active in women's groups and the YWCA. At university, she was part of the student struggle against apartheid – the most highly publicized campaign against institutional racism that the world has ever known. Then, like many young black activists, she was expelled. "You are not needed here," she was told.

Involved during the 1970s with Steve Biko and the Black Consciousness Movement, she kept away from the church, believing it to be politically irrelevant. Then in the 1980s she had the opportunity to attend a South African Council of Churches assembly on "Women – A Power for Change", and she realized the potential of the ecumenical movement to advance what came to be known as "The Struggle".

Her concern with women's issues came later, after the struggle against the political structures of apartheid had been won. As a woman, says Thoko Mpulwana, she grew up with the Decade, becoming a member of the WCC's commission on Justice, Peace and Creation and the moderator of the international planning group for the Decade Festival. So long as liberation from apartheid was the priority, men and women worked together, and women's issues were subordinated to the Struggle as a whole. But now it is different. South Africa, where institutional violence has reigned for so long, is facing new manifestations of violence against women. But women of colour *are* taking a more prominent role in the new South Africa, and Thoko Mpulwana herself had to leave Harare early in order to go home and work with the government on the registration of voters for the 1999 elections in South Africa.

From every other part of the world, as well, comes evidence of the tendency for the battle against racism to become the battle for the advancement of racially oppressed men, while women of colour remain doubly oppressed. From the USA: "Historically, this church has been a place where the African American male could express himself. Women have sacrificed their desire for leadership so that the men could have the opportunity to function in ways that are denied in the larger community." From Congo: "The political crisis tearing the country apart has reinforced tribal divisions..., and women and children are the first victims." From a Korean living in Japan: "Women in the church are facing a double struggle: for their identity and participation as

Koreans in Japan and as women in their church... All work together on discrimination against Koreans, but on discrimination against women we find little support."

In Britain, the ecumenical Churches' Commission for Racial Justice has worked courageously to change cultures and political structures of racism, both within society in general and within the church. Yet for me as an Englishwoman, many of the comments from my own country recorded in *Living Letters* are among the most depressing. On support for women under racism: "Sometimes it is easier to be in solidarity with oppressed women in other countries." And about Wales, itself conscious of being a racial minority within Britain, the dry observation of one team member: "They told us they have very little contact with immigrant communities." As one church leader said, "The church tends to get to social issues as a by-product." And again, the plight of minority-group women is subsumed under the more general struggle against racism.

Racial minority women studying or teaching in the white-male world of academic theology or theological education find themselves outsiders on two counts. "I had to learn a whole new language, a whole new set of codes," said a Brazilian *mujerista* theologian. "I was always terrified of giving myself away as an outsider. And then when I went home I had to try and remember who I really was."

The structures and worship of many churches are alienating for racial minority women. *Living Letters* contains some important insights. "A woman told us about having left the church to find alternative sources of worship and prayer, of being chastised and called primitive for going back to the traditional ways of her people." Many women of colour, doubly alienated by the male and majority spirituality and worship of the mainstream churches, have left these to form independent or house churches which speak to the spirituality of their own communities. Because many WCC member churches are often the ones of which they despair, and because these small house-church groups tend not to be formally represented in ecumenical organizations, the mid-Decade teams did not look at what is going on here. To do so would be a fascinating and illuminating exercise, from which we might all learn.

"Yes, Lord, but..."

The movement for racial equality has been one of the great social and political themes of the 20th century. The struggle against colonialism, which has turned upside down the political configuration of the world, was a struggle against global structures of racism.

Many churches are making strenuous efforts to rid themselves of the evils of racism. It is astonishing therefore to realize how difficult it still is for women and men to talk about racism in their own context. Mid-Decade teams were particularly struck by this in relation to the situation of *women* living under racism, and few of the churches visited could provide any data about progress made in advancing the position of minority-group women and girls.

In preparing the biblical study material for the Decade Festival, women from all regions were asked to submit imaginative contextual interpretations of biblical passages on the decade themes of violence against women, economic justice, racism and the participation of women in the churches. Very few chose to write theological reflections on the racism readings. Yet it is clear from personal testimonies that the pain of women who are doubly disadvantaged, first by being women, then by belonging to racial or ethnic minorities, is one of the great untold abuses of our time. Among its most flagrant manifestations is the recent increase in the trafficking of minority women and girls from poor countries to service the international sex industry. According to *Living Letters*:

> While many issues bring women into solidarity with each other, racism fragments that solidarity. Women of colour in many places report that the predominant women's movement does not address their concerns. In fact, it is not only men but also women of the majority culture who often discriminate against, exploit, exclude and oppress them on the basis on race... Some

church women's groups and movements do not recognize the
presence of racism, or refuse to recognize its importance, thus
confirming the accusations of indigenous, minority and black
women that women from the majority culture can be just as
oppressive as men (pp.29-30).

In working out why there appears to be such a taboo sur-
rounding this subject, it is worth looking back at the story of
the Syro-Phoenician or Canaanite woman, which seems to
speak particularly to women living in situations of racism
and to very poor women. Mark's and Matthew's gospels give
slightly different accounts of this incident, but they agree in
what they say about Jesus' own words and actions. Both
place this story immediately after a bruising confrontation
with the Jewish religious establishment, in which Jesus has
caused deep offence by publicly attacking the religious laws
on diet – traditions guarded jealously because they reinforced Jewish exclusiveness and superiority. "Listen to me,"
says Jesus in this encounter. "It is not what you eat that matters: that passes through you and goes into the drains. It is
what comes from the heart that is important." This argument
suggests that Jesus' mind was already focused on the scope
and nature of his ideal community, on who would be in and
who would be out. Hoping to avoid further confrontation and
have a bit of peace, Jesus gathers his disciples and they
retreat to the region around Tyre, which is in Gentile territory.

This is a controversial story, difficult to cope with, for
reasons made clear by Soon Ja Chung in her contribution to
the Decade Bible studies. First, Jesus' extreme rudeness is a
problem for Christians of all races, and women belonging to
racial minorities may find distressing and unacceptable his
reference to the woman's people as "dogs". And yet he does
back down and do what he has been asked – the only point
in all the gospels at which Jesus does not have the last word
but appears to have been persuaded by someone else's argument to change his mind. Some interpreters assert that Jesus
was only testing the woman's faith when he suggested that

her ethnic origins disqualified her daughter from his healing. What seems more likely is that Jesus really did learn from this encounter a new insight into what the kingdom of God was to be like. Brought up within Jewish culture, he had internalized the taboos, the attitudes and the discriminatory language expected of a Jewish man. Three things made him think again: the woman's verbal response, her love for her daughter and her faith that he would be able to help. It is not Jesus' weakness in changing his mind that we should focus on here, but his strength and intellectual honesty in being willing to restructure the whole pattern of assumptions which were his birthright as a Jewish male.

Traditional readings of this story assume that it is the woman's intelligence and her argumentative assertiveness which influence Jesus. But women who study this passage produce other interpretations. In judging that Jesus is primarily impressed by the woman's debating skills, some of them say, academic feminist theologians are feeding their own egos, reading into the story what they want to hear. On the contrary, they argue, it is the woman's faith, her need, and her love for her daughter which finally sway him. Both interpretations can be supported from the text. The earliest version of the story is the one in Mark's gospel, where Jesus tells the woman he will do as she asks "because of her word". Matthew's later version portrays Jesus as influenced by what is in the woman's heart, not by what she said. "Great is your faith," he says, and her little daughter is healed.

While this story speaks particularly to women living under racism, Elisabeth Schüssler Fiorenza suggests that the Syro-Phoenician woman (whom she calls Sophia) is in fact the prototype for all Gentile Christian women, claiming their place in God's kingdom by virtue of their faith, their resistance to exclusion, their powers of argument or their capacity for love.

Why does the woman not dispute Jesus' hurtful and insulting use of the word "dog"? Minority group women at the festival had no problem with that. This woman, they say, is overwhelmingly concerned for her daughter, driven by

Water in the Wilderness

(Genesis 16:1-16; 17:18-27; 21:1-21; 25:12-18)

Ten-year-old Hagar is excited when her mother tells
her she is to leave her home in Egypt and go to the land
of Canaan. At home drought has ruined the harvest
again. Already desperately poor, the family can now
barely scrape together enough food to keep them all
alive. There are just too many children. With the money
he gets for her, Hagar's father will be able to buy ten
goats.[1] And Hagar has always known she is meant for
something better. Her new master Abram, they say, is a
man of property, owning many sheep, and Hagar is to be
slave to his wife Sarai. So the next morning, as her
mother weeps and the younger children shout unwanted
advice, the young Hagar goes off with the bearded foreigner, head teeming with innocent thoughts of a future
full of promise.

To begin with, everything is fine. The little Egyptian
girl misses her home more than she expected to, but she
is bright and eager to please, and Sarai quickly becomes
fond of her. But Hagar can see that Sarai is often desperately unhappy. Despite all her prayers and offerings, she
has no child – a disgrace in itself, and for the family a disaster. She knows all about God's promise to her husband
Abram that he is to have descendants "more numerous
than the stars". But sometimes, these days, even Abram
seems to be losing hope.

The time comes when Sarai's monthly flow of
blood stops. It is the end. Her husband is dutiful
towards her; but equally, she knows that he must have
sons. He will have no choice but to take another wife,
unless. . . Sarai's eyes light on her pretty slave, who is
just coming to puberty. If a slave bears a child to her
master, that child may be counted as the legitimate
heir.[2] Better a pliable servant than another wife, thinks
Sarai. So one day she leads Hagar to the master's
chamber, turning away as the old man draws the little
slave-girl onto his sleeping mat and covers her with
his body. The sight of her husband mating with a
frightened child is not one Sarai wants to watch. But it
must be done. Hagar is her property, *she* has brought
her together with her husband and if a son is born it
will be *hers*.[3]

Hagar for her part is paralyzed with fear and shock. She tries to cry out, but no sound comes. Afterwards, what she remembers are his smell, the great rough hands on her body. Not being able to breathe. *The pain*. And then his sleeping weight, and the sudden terror that she will suffocate beneath him. Hoarsely, she cries out. He wakes, rolls over, stares at her in confusion, and then – not unkindly – he tells her to go. Legs buckling beneath her, she stumbles out and collapses on the ground behind the quarters of her mistress. She is eleven-and-a-half years old.

In due course, Hagar conceives. The pain and confusion of the rape are things of the past, and Hagar is beginning to enjoy being the patriarch's favourite. With her pregnancy, she is losing her child's body, and she enjoys his response to her beauty. She basks in the status of being his concubine. She always knew she was meant for something special: now, in all but law, she is a rich man's wife, and one day she will be the mother of his children. Sarai, who has been kind to her, is yesterday's woman: hardly a woman even, unable as she is to satisfy her husband or bear his children.

Hagar, though, is not old enough or wise enough to hide these thoughts from Sarai, who is, after all, still her mistress. Now Sarai cannot remember why she wanted this harlot's child. Her bitterness and fury rise till she thinks she will choke on them; and when her husband comes home, she offers him an ultimatum. Choose, she says. This girl is a slave and must be taught a lesson. And Abram, whose dislike of "troubles between women" is even greater than his growing affection for Hagar, says, "She is your slave: do what you like with her."[4] So Sarai and her women take Hagar and beat her, and when the girl comes to herself, she knows she must leave this place or risk being killed.

Bruised and pregnant, Hagar stumbles out into the desert. She has allowed herself to dream of freedom. How stupid! The reality of life is that it is about men and power, family and inheritance. As a woman, the story of her life will always be a scribble in the margin. As a servant, womb and all, she only matters as far as they are able to make use of her. As a homeless, penniless for-eigner, she is little more than an animal waiting at the door for scraps. She comes to a spring of water and sinks down beside it. Egypt and home: she will never see them again. Death is the only freedom she is ever likely to know. Heavy with weeping, gritty with sand, her eyes close.

Time passes. The life within her stirs and kicks. And a voice seems to say, "Hagar, slave-girl of Sarai, where are you coming from and where are you going?" She opens her eyes, but there is no one. She has never thought of herself as a slave, no matter what others might call her. Can it be that her own thoughts are now betraying her? Again the voice comes: "Hagar, you are going to have to go back into the power of your mistress." *I cannot*, says her heart, *or I will die*. But the voice persists: "I will so greatly multiply your offspring that they cannot be counted for the multitude. It is for the generations to come that you must go back, not just yourself."

And at this moment Hagar knows without any doubt that she is in the presence of God. She is not invisible. However hideous her life may be, it matters whether she lives or dies. She raises her eyes, and the parched land is filled with a presence. "You are *El-roi*!", she cries out in wonderment.[5] "You are the one who sees, the living one who sees me." The moment passes, but the wonder stays. It is deep inside her being, closer than her womb, more alive than the life within her. Painfully, she clam-bers to her feet and turns her face back towards Abram's home. She is too exhausted to move fast. She dreads the humiliating return, the certainty of punishment. She has no illusions: in choosing life, she has chosen suffering. Nothing has changed.

But *she* has changed. Aloud, knowing the answer before she asks, she cries into the desert wind, "Can it be true that I have seen God and remained alive after seeing him?"

So Hagar goes back to Sarai. Eventually, the baby is born. It is a boy, Ishmael, and for a while, he is the son and heir. As nursing mother of the master's child, she is partly protected from Sarai's bitterness and violence. But

God's promises are not always what they seem. Hagar has not foreseen that Sarah herself will conceive at last. Ishmael will father a nation, but Sarah's son Isaac, born in her old age, will become the bearer of the promise of the covenant.

When Isaac is eight days old, the proud father holds a feast to celebrate his son's circumcision. Pausing in her duties as a hostess, Sarah notices Hagar playing happily with the baby. The girl is her husband's concubine, the mother of the child who is her own infant son's rival. What if she were to harm him? Overwhelmed with jealousy, fearful for her child, Sarah begs the reluctant Abraham to get rid of Hagar, and his elder son Ishmael. Once again Hagar finds herself cast out into the desert, this time with her little boy.[6]

This time, however, there is no return. The water Abraham has given them soon runs out. As far as they can see, there is nothing but scrub and rocks, the endless, windswept sand and the merciless sun above. Before they starve, they will die of dehydration. The child cannot walk far, he is heavy in her arms, and soon she herself will have to rest. Hopeless, unable to bear the thought of watching her son die, Hagar settles him gently in the shade of a scraggy bush. She walks until she can hear his howls no longer, then sinks down on the ground and gives herself over to despair. When Ishmael is dead, she will bury him, and then, here in the desert, she will lie down and die herself.

Then, out of the depths of her grief, she hears once again the voice of El-roi, the God who sees. "Do not be afraid," the voice says. Opening her tired eyes, Hagar sees before her a spring of water. Why has she not noticed it before? Here in the wilderness, the God who sees has given her the ability to find resources for survival, even in this most desperate situation, when everything seems finally to be lost.

Finally, we see Hagar, now a free woman, seeking a bride for her son Ishmael among her own, Egyptian people.[7]

NOTES

[1] This was a common reason for selling a girl into slavery, as it is today.

[2] The Hurrian family code allowed sterile wives to give their slaves as concubines to their husbands and then claim the offspring as their own.

[3] Cf. Musimbi Kanyoro's comments on "Interpreting Old Testament Polygamy through African Eyes", in *The Will to Arise: Women, Tradition and the Church in Africa,* Mercy A. Oduyoye and Musimbi Kanyoro, eds, Maryknoll NY, Orbis, 1992.

[4] The Code of Hammurabi imposed a penalty on slaves who as concubines tried to gain equal status with the legal wife.

[5] Hagar is the first woman to "name" God and the first to be told that she is part of God's plans.

[6] According to the law, the concubine's child should be equal to the child of the wife as far as inheritance is concerned. In effect, Sarah obeys the law when it suits her, but ignores it when it is convenient to do so.

[7] The history of Ishmael's descendants, the Ishmaelites, would come to be interwoven with the history of the children of Israel, who despised them.

5. Your Story is My Story

We were told
yes, there is violence
but not in our circles
not in the church
not in Christian homes.

We almost believed it.
But then we started to listen
and the church got another face.

We learned what we did not want to believe
we heard what we could hardly bear.

We know now
there is violence against women in our very midst
in the churches
in Christian homes.

We know now
that violence against women
exists in the church
is ignored by the church
is even justified by the church

We know now
that violence against women
happens in our very midst.

Irja Askola

Ask anyone involved with the Ecumenical Decade what is the most urgent "stone to be rolled away" and the answer is likely to be "violence against women in church and society". Written in the early years of the Decade, Aruna Gnanadasan's *No Longer a Secret* paints a chilling picture of the personal, sexual, political, cultural, racial and economic violence women encounter in every part of the world. The reports of the mid-Decade team visits in *Living Letters* speak of a universal climate of violence against women, both inside and outside the church, and the equally universal silence in which it is shrouded. The revised edition of *No Longer a Secret,* published in 1997, summarizes the Decade's findings on the subject of violence against women, and sets out the theological and ecclesiological challenges which emerge from them.

Between 1993 and 1996, the WCC organized meetings on violence against women in every region of the world, and the findings of these have been collected in a publication called *Together with Courage*. Bible study material prepared for the Festival in Harare – *A Decade of Solidarity with the Bible* – contains powerful reflections from all over the world on the stories of Hagar (Gen. 16), Rizpah (2 Sam. 21) and the unnamed concubine (Judg. 19) who was offered by her host to the neighbours, who gang-raped her and left her to die.

For many who were present at the Decade Festival itself, it was the sessions dealing with women's testimonies of violence that struck the most painful and memorable chords. Olivia Juarez, whom we cited in the previous chapter, speaks of the violence experienced by indigenous women, and in particular the violence which results from the suppression of their history. Susan, from Aotearoa New Zealand, spoke of experiencing institutional violence against women, in a church which claims to practise openness and fairness. Of the many voices, we shall listen to four in this chapter – Rebecca from Papua New Guinea, Ann from Canada, Hannah from Kenya, and Ada Maria from the USA.

* * *

Rebecca's story struck a resonance for many women. Rebecca comes from a strong Roman Catholic background. At 17 she was married to a man she hardly knew. The marriage lasted six years – six years of hell – during which few days passed without an episode of drunkenness and violence. Active in the church, she went to the priest with her troubles. He responded with embarrassment. "You must be patient, and understand your husband's problems," he said. "Go home and cook him a nice dinner." Some weeks later, she went back to the priest, this time with a black eye and a broken arm. "God made women to be patient," he said. "Jesus suffered on the cross for you: can you not stand a little suffering for him?"

One evening her husband came home particularly drunk. Rebecca swears that the only reason he did not kill her that night was because he tripped and fell, and was overtaken by sleep before he could get up. She was rescued by a friend, who offered her refuge. But the priests at her church have continued to say that she should never have left her husband. "Go home, dear," she was told. "You will bring your family into disrepute, and probably the church as well." In fact, Rebecca was taken in by the kind friend who rescued her, and in the course of time she applied to have her marriage annulled.

That happened 22 years ago. For many years, Rebecca has been living with the friend who saved her life. But the church is still dragging its feet over an annulment, and for all those 22 years she has been excluded from the sacraments. She finds this deeply painful. "It is shameful," she says, "to sit down while others receive the body and blood of Christ." Meanwhile, the man who almost murdered her is allowed to partake, while the one who took her in and cared for her is not. And there have been widely publicized stories of priests who keep mistresses but nevertheless continue to celebrate the eucharist.

As Rebecca tells her story, it is clear that her pain at the total inability of the church to understand or help her deal with her problems is as raw as ever. She still asks herself whether she should have stayed in the marriage and let herself be killed. Yet Rebecca loves her church. She has never wanted to be anywhere else. God is present in its sacraments through God's own grace, she says. However weak and sinful we are, that grace has the power to transform and redeem. Where do we find that kind of generosity of spirit and understanding of human frailty reflected in the church? "Perhaps when it is dealing with priests," says Rebecca bitterly, "but not when it's dealing with women."

When Rebecca finished her story, there was a moment's silence. Many women had tears in their eyes. "Your story is my story," they said gently. "Your story is *our* story."

* * *

Ann is a Canadian, the daughter of an Anglican priest. Her father was a high-church Anglo-Catholic with a strong sense of hell and damnation, who would preach terrifying sermons about God's anger. The sexual abuse began when she was very small, and Ann never quite sorted out the difference between God and her father. As with God, she feared him, but she also adored him. She was his special little girl, and what he did to her was their special secret.

When she was seven, her father "came to Christ" at a charismatic rally. Eventually he became involved with what Ann calls "The Group". When Ann's brother died, The Group persuaded her father to try to get in touch with the boy, and Ann was summoned back from college to help contact him. Coerced into joining The Group, she found they were soon dominating her life. They regulated her university course, told her what to wear, how to behave, and eventually whom to marry. If anything went wrong, the devil was always blamed. There were exorcisms and beatings of members who were sick or disturbed or who had disobeyed one or another of the many rules. When Ann became engaged, her father undressed her, conducted what he called a "ritual eucharistic anointing" and dressed her in a long white gown. Her fiancé was then called, and her father watched while he had sex with her.

The crisis came when Katy, a member of The Group, contracted meningitis. This, she was told, was the devil attacking her. She was not allowed to go to the hospital. There were public beatings and exorcisms, and Katy died. Ann's father was tried, found negligent (but not criminal) and lost his licence. When Ann finally decided to leave home, he threw her downstairs.

Not surprisingly, Ann believes she will never fully recover from the effects of her relationship with her father. She has fought to find acceptance in the church. She has struggled to reclaim the church rituals that were used against her. But it has been difficult. She has problems with the patriarchal structures of the church which she has joined. But she knows she must keep going, and she is getting stronger all the time. What she is still unable to understand is how such things could go on, for so long, within the so-called Christian church, and everybody could turn a blind eye.

* * *

Hannah comes from a rural area in Kenya. Her father died from what she now believes was AIDS, and his parents sent her mother back to her own parents, along with the younger children. Because Hannah was in her last year of school, she went to live with her uncle and aunt, who had no children of their own. On her first night in his house, and every night for the next few months, her uncle came to her room and raped her. Within weeks, she found that she was pregnant.

Hannah continued to go to school until the pregnancy started to show. Then she was sent to live with cousins in Nairobi, where her son Joseph was eventually born. When he was four days old, her uncle and aunt came to Nairobi and took him away. She has never seen him since. She tried to go back and visit, but her uncle said he would kill her if she ever came near their home again. Later she realized what had happened: her aunt had faked pregnancy during the months while Hannah was carrying Joseph, and today the couple are passing him off as their own child. Hannah still believes she will one day be reunited with her little boy, that he will one day know her for his mother. In her heart, she says, she will never give him up.

In the meantime, she has been lucky. Her school was run by an order of nuns. Realizing that there was a college in Nairobi belonging to the same order, she went one day to see if they could help her find one of her old teachers, who had been kind to her in the past. They took her in, she sat the exams she had missed and was admitted to a Catholic teacher's training college.

Now Hannah is a trainee teacher herself. She is fond of a young man who is a youth leader in her church. She sometimes sees one of her sisters, and sends money when she can to her mother to help with the support of the other children. But her first thought when she wakes and her last thought at night is of the little boy she has not seen since he was four days old.

* * *

Ada Maria is a teacher of theology and a pastor. As a woman and a member of an ethnic minority group, she is filled with rage at the violence she sees in the USA against women theologians. Theology, she says, should be a critique of culture, a cry for justice. But when women use theology to make a critique of the culture of academic theology, they are silenced, ignored and made fun of. The Prodigal Son in Jesus' parable (Luke 15) was a man, she observes. What would have happened if he had been a woman? Women, she answers, are rarely given a second chance, never given the benefit of the doubt.

One Easter Sunday, she says, there was a flu epidemic, and all available clergy, including her academic colleagues who were not in pastoral posts, were taking services in as many churches as they had time for. Ordained women who were members of her department were not asked to be part of the emergency support team. You are scholarly, they were told, so you are not part of the community. You are an active feminist, so you are not in touch with women in the pews. You are a woman, so you will not be welcome as a visiting preacher.

Ada Maria sees the problem as a theological one. Activism has its place, she says, but it can be counter-productive; it can produce the opposite of what you want to achieve. As long as the God of academic theology is recognized solely through the experience of men, and described only through male imagery and thinking, women will continue to be outsiders in academic and leadership roles in the churches.

A culture of silence

It is beyond the scope of this book to review the full range of the Decade's findings on violence against women. This is well-documented, with the available literature demonstrating that violence against women is an everyday experience in most cultures. It is also one of the biggest untold secrets of our time. Any woman who has lived in a violent relationship knows it: being on the receiving end of regular bullying and violence is a deeply humiliating and private matter. It is not so much the pain as the violation of the whole personality. Where the violence is physical, the experience of being struck or beaten, particularly by someone to whom one is close, has about it a horrifying intimacy which goes beyond the intimacy of sex. The relationship between abused and abuser becomes a macabre dance which pervades the whole of one's life. Some years ago, British television screened a documentary on violence against women. It was entitled "Don't Scream Too Loud – The Neighbours Will Hear You". Both are locked into it by a conspiracy of silence. It is all too easy to lose track of reality altogether and take refuge in depression and neurosis – and for many suicide is the final movement in the dance.

The problem with conspiracies of silence is that objective data tend to be scarce. The Decade teams went looking for them, and these are some of the stories they heard. From India: "We heard pathetic stories of dowry deaths, bride burnings and suicides. We learned that these things happen even in Christian families. We heard of ostracism of widows by their close relatives – even among Christians, where the installation of elders was originally an effort to bring justice to widowed women." From South Africa: "Wife beating is a common practice. The beatings range from hitting to beating with a stick, to stabbing, to injury which leads to death. Women of all ages, colour and socio-economic levels are victims of physical and sexual abuse." From the USA: "A priest was found to be abusing young girls. It was all hushed up and he was transferred to another parish." And so on, through every region of the world.

Most worrying of all has been the realization of the prevalence of violence in the church itself, and the complicity of the church in covering it up. From the Czech Republic:

"Most churches said there is no violence against women *except among the Gypsies...* But we heard that it is widespread, with women being forced into prostitution and white-slave trafficking." From Argentina: "The church does not deal with family problems, because we present an ideal picture of the family as in the gospel. We do not discuss the fundamental problems. We do not get to where it hurts."

There was a remarkable uniformity about how church leaders in different regions replied when asked about violence against women. They often asserted that violence was something that happens "out there", in the community outside the church, denying that it was an issue in the lives of church members or clergy. More often, in speaking with clergy and church leaders, Decade teams encountered attempts at justification. "It's part of our culture" was a common response. Some felt that violence resulting in death should be distinguished from "just hitting". One leader spoke of "disciplining" his wife and being thanked by her afterwards. In one church, clergy said they were opposed to violence "except in certain circumstances". Several spoke of physical punishment as "helping women to achieve salvation". Pastorally, the norm seems to be for clergy to advise women to go back to a violent situation, to put up with it, not to rock the boat.

Most depressing of all was the apparent complicity of women themselves, and their readiness to accept that violence against them was justified, even condoned by the Bible. Take the priest's injunction to Rebecca: "Jesus suffered for you: can you not bear a little suffering for his sake?" Suffering with Christ, turning the other cheek, living for others: these were offered as the way for women to achieve salvation within a Christian society. Is it the way for men to achieve salvation too? Is violence by stronger Christians against weaker Christians to be recommended? What an extraordinary piece of theological sleight of hand, when applied to the teaching of the Christ whose blueprint for human relationships included love, joy, gentleness, goodness and holiness.

The God who sees

The story of Hagar has been a key text for the Decade. It seems to resonate with women from every region. Hagar's experiences, with all their horror, continue in every migrant worker deprived of personal power, every maid who is oppressed by another woman, every lone mother who is cast out with her child and left to fend for herself, every teenage girl who is flattered, raped and discarded by an older man, every woman used as a surrogate child-bearer, every woman who is an outsider to a religious tradition but nevertheless claims her legitimate role in the history of God's purposes.

Perhaps more than any other biblical narrative, the story of Hagar highlights the complex nature of violence against women. Hagar is a victim of economic, racial, religious and cultural violence. She is far from home, sold by her family into slavery. She is raped by her master. She is living in a culture where surrogacy is accepted. It is a tale of abuse, despair and failure in which the poor and powerless come off worst, and the oppressors get everything they want. There is no liberation, no neat, satisfactory ending.

Normally, this story is read through the perspective of the dominant narrative, which is the history of God's chosen people. Abraham is a patriarch, the great patriarchal figure of Judaeo-Christian tradition. The story of Hagar and Sarah is the tale of two women locked into a patriarchal system. Abraham is given the opportunity to alter the course of events. Instead, he acquiesces to each of Sarah's requests: that Hagar should bear his child (which was permitted by the law), that he sanction violence against her (also allowed by the law) and that Hagar and the boy be sent away after Isaac's birth (which was not in keeping with the law). Hagar was, if you like, a casualty of "the system", but she was also a victim of those who were in a position to manipulate the system for their own purposes.

Tradition and history have not been kind to Hagar. During her life, she was used and abused by others in the interests of their own ambitions. Her descendants, though children of Abraham, were despised by the people of Israel and treated as aliens. Christian tradition has associated Hagar with enslavement and the sins of the flesh – Christians, on the other hand, being the natural inheritors of freedom and the spirit, represented by Sarah. Hence, in his discussion of circumcision, Paul assures the community at Galatia that they as Christians are "children not of the slave but of the free woman" (Gal. 4:31).

In *Texts of Terror,* US theologian Phyllis Trible concludes her telling of the desolation of Hagar with the insight that she is a contrasting, mirror image of Israel's pilgrimage of faith. "As a maid in bondage," says Trible, "she flees from suffering. Yet she experiences exodus without liberation, revelation without salvation, wilderness without covenant, wanderings without land, promise without fulfilment, and unmerited exile without return."

For all that, this story inspired some of the most powerful biblical writing to emerge from the Decade. Hagar is the first biblical woman to name God, and to receive a divine message. As many abused and unhappy women point out, the angel's instruction to "return to your mistress and submit to her", while it is nothing more than a strategy for survival at the most minimal level, is also nothing *less* than that, and sometimes survival is the best that can be managed. Further, Hagar receives a second message on that first encounter. In promising her that she will become the mother of a nation, the angel is also saying, in effect, "There is a place for you in God's purposes, so the pain of survival is not for nothing." On Hagar's second encounter with the angel, she learns to find, in her own wilderness environment, the basic resources that will enable her to survive and raise her child alone.

Read from the perspective of its casualties, this story is a particularly powerful one for women. Hong Kong theologian Kwok Pui-Lan comments: "It seems that African Americans focus on Hagar as a slave woman, the Latin Americans stress that she was poor, the Africans underscore the face of Hagar in polygamy, and Asians emphasize the loss of cultural identity. Each group observes a certain analogy between the oppression of Hagar and their own situation."

It is worth noting that patriarchal structures seem to breed violence against women. Anthropologists point out that rape is almost unknown in matrilineal societies, where violence against women is considered socially and culturally unacceptable. This cultural norm seems to be stronger than the religious tradition, since it holds true even where the dominant religion is a patriarchal one, as in Muslim West Sumatra.

In talking with the members of the teams which took part in the mid-Decade visits, I have observed that men and women responded differently to reports of violence against women. For women, it was what they knew or suspected already. For men, the stories of violence and the responses of the church leaders came as a shock. One man described what can only be called a conversion experience, when he suddenly "saw the point". Another spoke of the deep shame he felt at the behaviour of some male church leaders they met, and at the violence they sanctioned in their churches. Several said how moved they were by the courage of those men who risked marginalization in their own male culture in order to stand with women.

"Violence against women is an ecclesiological question," states Aruna Gnanadasan in the preamble to *Together with Courage*. "It is a threat to the very being of the churches. It is not simply a women's issue, but is an integral concern of both women and men, lay and clergy. Violence against women threatens the witness and identity of the churches as caring communities of shared power. By their silence, the churches deny themselves their authority as moral agents of justice and dignity for all God's people."

One of the Decade's greatest gifts has been a fractional loosening of that culture of silence, both among women themselves and within institutional churches, councils of churches and regional bodies. Groups in different regions are organizing and lobbying: the Circle of Concerned African Women Theologians; in Taiwan, the Centre for Trafficked Women; the international Sisters Network, bringing together the concerns of women living under racism. In Norway, the churches themselves have set up a centre for addressing violent attitudes and behaviour in their own ranks. The Conference of European Churches is currently organizing a major initiative on trafficked women.

For churches and church organizations wondering where to begin, here are some general principles, which might prove helpful as a basis for discussion.

First, there is a need for a continued growth in solidarity among women, and churches must provide opportunities for this to take place in safety. In practice, this is already happening in some places. Women are becoming more willing to talk to each other. The need for refuges and support groups for battered women and girls is being accepted, and in some places this has become a priority for the churches.

Second, there is need for willingness by clergy to reassess pastoral practice in the support of families. Sexuality and violence are a legitimate concern for those involved in theological and clergy education, and also as part of in-service training. In some parts of the world, faced by the devastation of whole communities by AIDS, churches have recognized the need (which may be culturally alien) for women to be free to control their own sexuality as a major element in the struggle against HIV. As a result, gender issues are already beginning to feature in the curricula of clergy education.

Third, there is a need for a determined effort on the part of church structures to see that abuse by clergy no longer remains hidden. High-profile examples of clergymen and priests accused or convicted of sexual violence have made it impossible any longer to maintain the fiction that this does not occur. Painful as it is, the church has no moral credibility in dealing with these issues if it does not at least attempt to put its house in order.

But whatever programmatic steps are taken, they will not get to the heart of the problem until men as well as women are able to look at the theological and ecclesiological basis of violence against women. They need to do this separately as well as together. This is an intensely difficult issue for concerned men, as well as for women. The way we habitually read the scriptures, the way we instinctively approach issues of hierarchy in the churches, the very language we use in the liturgy may all be contributing to the maintenance of an ecclesial culture in which violence against women is condoned. As Konrad Raiser said in Harare, at the end of the session on violence, "Only the church that admits the sickness can be healed." Violence against women is a sin. If the church is implicated in it, then it is for men as well as women to put it right. To do so would create a better church for all of us. But the biggest and most painful effort will have to come from the men.

The water of survival

In Hagar's story, and in many of the other stories in this chapter, it is easy to see nothing but unrelenting violence. Nevertheless Hagar, victim as she is, has a prophetic role in history. It is not just for herself and her child that she is called to survive. Rather, she is the first in a long and honourable line of biblical characters who go out into the desert and find God. In this, she is the prototype for Jacob, Moses and the whole people of Israel, for Elijah, and eventually for Jesus himself. Abused by a patriarch, she becomes the first matriarch, promised by God that her descendants will have a place in history, challenged to survive for the sake of the generations to come.

Hagar is the prototype for all those women who struggle on, called to be part of a wilderness community, called to be faithful for our own sakes and for the sakes of those who come after. Sometimes, as in Hagar's case, survival will dictate that they go back into the oppressive situation; sometimes they will need to move on. In either case, this story brings the assurance of streams of living water springing up in the wilderness for those who are given the grace to see.

The Flame of God

(The Song of Solomon)

As an old, old woman, she remembered it still, that spring of passion. Dreaming in the sun, under the old apple tree, she would stop her children's children in their games, to tell them the now-familiar story. And they would gaze in disbelief at the bent frame, the faded, wispy hair, the watery eyes, and they would ask themselves how it could possibly be true.

But for Shula,[1] who has difficulty now in remembering what happened yesterday, it is as sharp as if she were still young, and the time of courting were today. She has only to shut her eyes and he is with her again, her beautiful love. Her lips are warm with his kisses, her body remembers the urgency of his longing for her. It is *that year* once more. She has been out working in the family vineyards, and she is black and beautiful, burned dark by the sun. All day she thinks of him. Where does he take his flock? She longs to know. But he loves playing games, and he sets a test for her, telling her to follow the tracks of his sheep to where he is.

And of course she finds him, as he longs to be found. She is lying now among the lilies, on a couch of green. He has been feeding her with raisins and slices of apple, lying there with the sun filtering through the green boughs above. Their love has constructed a world of its own, in which their very bodies speak to the glory of creation. Mere words are too weak to tell their passion. *His hair is black and glossy as a raven, his body tall, strong, like the cedars of Lebanon... My breasts are fawns, my hair like a flock of goats streaming down the mountain, my cheeks like the pomegranate halves...* His left arm is beneath her head; his other hand is tracing tender patterns on her throat, her breasts, her belly, until her whole body aches with his touch. "I am a rose of Sharon," she whispers, "a lily of the valleys..."

She is suddenly cautious.[2] *Love has its own pace*, she thinks. *Let it take its time* – advice she has since given to her daughters and grand-daughters, though they take little notice.

Shula is asleep, but her heart is awake and waiting. Now she is in her childhood bed, in her mother's house. And listen! Her beloved is knocking. Urgent and demanding, his whisper comes out of the night. "Open to me, my sister, my love, my dove, my perfect one." But by the time she gets to the window, he has gone, and there is sweet-smelling ointment all over the handle. Oh, his jokes, and his constant teasing... Faint with love, her soul failing within her, she follows him, but even the guards have not seen him. How is she to know that he has gone to his sheep, pastured among the lilies?

He calls her "sister" now. If he were really her brother, she could kiss him in public, bring him to her mother's house, give him the juice of her pomegranates to drink, take him to her room. *Stop!*, she thinks. *Do not stir up or awaken love until it is ready.*

So the spring passes. The flowers appear on the earth, the voice of the turtle dove is heard, the fig tree puts forth figs. "Come, my beloved," she murmurs one day. "Let us go out into the fields, and lodge in the villages; let us go out early to the vineyards and see whether the grapes have budded. And there I will give you my love, the fruits which I have kept for you, O my love."

It is her free choice, to give herself to him.[3] *My vineyard, my body's love, is for myself, for me to give*, she whispers. *My beloved is mine, and I am his.*

* * *

Usually, at this point, she wakes up, making the painful transition from past reality to the dreamlike present. Today, she lingers in sleep. Waking means leaving him. His kisses have been sweeter today, his words more urgent. Her frail old flesh throbs with the memory. *I will arise now*, she murmurs. *I will go about the city, in the streets and in the squares; I will seek him whom my soul loves.*

And then he is here, under the tree, in among the sun-streaked shade *"I come to my garden, my sister, my bride..."* Across the years his voice is calling. *My beloved is mine, and his desire is for me...* His presence surrounds her, like the scent of myrrh; his summons is growing more urgent. "*Awake, my love, my dear one, and come away...*

Into her heart comes flooding all the love she has known for him in life, a great fierce flame, strong as death itself. *Many waters cannot quench love:* back from the past, the words come pouring. The pain in her chest expands. *Make haste, my beloved.* And deep inside the pain, she finds him – and the other men and the women and all the children she has loved in her long life: those she has been able to love because of her love for him. She knows it now, her life has taught her this: that human passion is made of the same stuff as the energy which created the universe. It is the flame of God,[4] and in the midst of it we touch hands with the eternal.

The old heart hesitates. Stops. Gentle as snow, the apple blossom settles on the thin hair. The time of singing has come, and around her, like little foxes,[5] the children go on playing.

As the warmth leaves the day, it is the adults who find her, there under the old tree, and marvel because she looks so peaceful.

NOTES

[1] In the Song of Solomon, she is called "the Shulamite". The word probably relates to the name Solomon, and also to *shalom*, meaning wholeness, or peace, so we could call her "the peaceful one". It could also refer to Sulmanitu, a Mesopotamian goddess, or to a woman from Shunem (1 Kings 1:1-4).

[2] "I adjure you, O daughters of Jerusalem..., do not stir up or awaken love until it is ready!" (S. of S. 2:7; 5:8).

[3] S. of S. 8:12. She is making a free disposal of herself to her lover, an attitude in keeping with 8:7b, which disdains the bride price.

[4] Cf. S. of S. 8:6.

[5] In the New Jerome Biblical Commentary, R.E. Murphy suggests that the little foxes are her other suitors.

6. The Great Taboos

In late November 1998 there are some 25 wars going on in different parts of the world. In Africa, Asia and Latin America, currencies are collapsing. In the Balkans, regions are being "ethnically cleansed". In North America and Britain, air forces are preparing for renewed bombing missions against Iraq. But what is dominating the news is not the fate of nations, the plight of the global economy or the organized atrocities being committed against entire peoples. Instead – hour after hour, page after page – it is detailed, explicit accounts of the sexual behaviour of the President of the United States.

Meanwhile, in Zimbabwe, the former president has been convicted of sexual offences against boys and young men, and the current president declares homosexuality to be a moral abomination. At the Lambeth Conference of Anglican bishops in August, the subject most widely reported in the media was its bitter divisions over the issue of homosexuality.

Some incidents from the Decade Festival, where the issue of sexuality surprised everyone by becoming a contentious one:

1. During the Festival there are two moving and beautifully presented sessions on violence against women. Lesbian groups point out that there was no lesbian speaker on the panel, so the experience of *homosexual* women was not specifically addressed. And yet there is a wealth of evidence – from the Caribbean, South Africa, Germany, Eastern Europe and elsewhere – of lesbian women being victimized and marginalized, both in churches and in society at large.

2. A young woman who is a leading member of Gays and Lesbians of Zimbabwe (GALZ) stands up and addresses the whole Festival. For her courageous and honest account of her own experiences as a Zimbabwean lesbian, she gets a standing ovation.

3. No hut has been specifically designated as a meeting place for lesbian women. Nevertheless, there is opportunity for ongoing dialogue in the Violence Against Women hut and the Theology hut. Organizers had a well-founded fear that

there would be protests, especially from African women. "But African women were very interested," says Herta Leistner. "Some of them kept coming back. Also, they were very direct. 'What do you actually *do*?', they kept asking. By being here, we are showing solidarity with Zimbabwean lesbians."

4. In an effort to acknowledge the difficulties that exist while avoiding confrontation, the final report uses the phrase "sexuality in all its diversity", as an inclusive term to communicate that both heterosexual and homosexual relationships are being referred to, but without using the taboo word "lesbian". Noting that "sexuality in all its diversity" is "difficult to address in the church community", the report goes on to say that this has "implications for participation" – which presumably means that there are some churches which would withdraw from any organization which took sides over it.

In the event, this careful wording does not fool anyone. There are protests from Middle Eastern women that this will be understood by their own church leaders as a coded way of expressing approval of homosexual relationships. From African women come further objections. "I have no problems with this matter myself," says a woman from the Democratic Republic of Congo, "but homosexuality is a controversial issue, it is not part of our culture, and we should have been warned in advance if we were going to be expected to take a position on it."

5. A prominent African churchwoman says, "They know it is going on, but they do not want to face up to it, so they just hide their heads in the sand."

6. A quotation from a white woman from the midwestern United States, in response to the Council's refusal to ban homosexual participation or to limit the participation of homosexual Christian groups: "Was this the hidden agenda all the time?", she asks. "Because in that case, I have been cheated and I should never have come."

Tina and Herta, whose stories follow, come from very different contexts.

"I feel sick when I smell herbs"

Because of evidence that government secret police were present at seminars discussing issues of sexuality at the assembly, I met Tina by a swimming pool, where we could talk in private. A prominent member of GALZ, she is a warm, vulnerable woman who looks much younger than her 30 years.

Tina was still at college, training to be a mechanic, when she admitted to her parents that she was a lesbian. Her father beat her up. Believing that she was mentally ill, her parents took her to a psychiatrist, to a traditional healer, to faith healers. "Today when I smell herbs I feel sick," she says. *Having a child will cure her*, they said; and they made her get engaged to a man who then moved into their home and raped her.

GALZ is now ten years old. "For us, in this country," says Tina, "the work has just begun." GALZ has no facilities, and they cannot organize counselling services because they are not permitted to advertise: in Zimbabwe, female homosexuality comes under the Unnatural Offences Law. GALZ has tried to hold seminars in churches, and people were keen to attend. Some were genuinely interested, some came to ridicule, some to picket. Most pastors are hostile, though, and recently, a group of Zimbabwean churches put an advertisement in the papers which said in effect that homosexual men should be castrated. "And Zimbabwean Christians listen to their churches," says Tina.

She continues with her own story. "When I left the church, I thought I would never touch a Bible again. But the New Testament has so much to say about kindness and loving each other. Now I have a kind of church in my own home. On Sunday, my friends come and we watch television together and sing. Sometimes they have a Christian *braai* – the Southern African barbecue – at the GALZ centre, and sing church songs. There is one priest who wants to start a gay church, but he is not 'out', and he is scared."

In some ways, says Tina, GALZ is her life. But there is a hierarchy in the movement. "The guys are still the bosses," she says. "The men are brought up to lead, and the women end up killing themselves." Three of her lesbian friends have committed suicide in the past three years. In Zimbabwe, all lesbians experience violence of one kind or another. Currently GALZ is trying to find premises for a safe house for lesbians, but non-governmental organizations fear that supporting GALZ might cost them their own government accreditation.

When Tina returned to her home after addressing the Festival, she discovered that her landlady's sister had been among the women in the audience. "Out with you!", said the landlady, throwing her possessions into the street.

"What will you do?", I ask.

"I have wonderful friends," Tina says. And I think to myself that I have rarely met such a mixture of courage and vulnerability, caution and kindness.

For 19 years Herta Leistner worked in the Protestant Academy in Bad Boll in southern Germany, where she started a lesbian visibility programme. She remembers that 40 people attended her first annual conference. Now they have 250 every year. There are networks of lesbian theologians and students, and their newsletter goes to fourteen countries, including Japan, the Philippines, Fiji and South Africa.

Herta says she is disappointed that the Festival excluded the lesbian experience of violence. "But never mind," she says. "We have experience of exclusion. We understand." She talks of her own struggles. At Bad Boll she produced a publication called *Lesbianism and the Church.* Conservatives in the church tried to get her appointment reviewed, and when that failed they put her photo in the newspaper. Six months later, she found her programme was in danger of losing its financial support.

"The Decade has been very helpful," says Herta. "The issues were there already, but now it was possible to raise them in reference to the Decade. Still, at the end of the day, it is our life, and we have to claim it. Otherwise we have to leave the church."

Today, Herta runs a women's academy in Northern Germany. She talks coolly and dispassionately about the plight of lesbians in Germany. "That," she says, "is the way it is." But the stories she tells me from Jamaica, Fiji and Romania make me realize what courage it takes to "come out", anywhere, as a lesbian woman, and what a challenge this is to global solidarity and communication. In the case of fragile groups like GALZ, it is up to women from less pressured societies and more protected situations to help in any way they can.

The Greatest Song

In Hebrew, the title "Song of Songs" means "the greatest of all songs", or "the song to end all songs". Passionate and erotic, this short book is about human sexual love, expressed mainly in a dialogue between two lovers. In spite of some early opposition, the Song of Songs is canonical for Christians from Roman Catholic, Orthodox and Protestant traditions, and also for Jews. In Jewish liturgy, it was traditionally read on the Feast of the Passover.

The most remarkable thing about the Song of Songs is the fact that it is in the Bible at all. I was brought up to think that including it in the canon was something of an aberration, and that the whole thing was an elaborate allegory for the love of God. Most scholars today seem to agree that it should be read literally, as a real experience of sexual love and courtship, to be taken seriously in its own right. The God of Israel had no female consort, was not a sexual being. Human eroticism, it seems, needed no mystical or divine counterpart in order to make it good.

What the Song provides is a biblical model for specifically human intimacy. Passion is there, and delight in the physical beauty of the other. It is a highly-charged *physical* relationship that is being described. But mutuality, fidelity, devotion, caution and a serious commitment to the relationship are also stressed. "Set me as a seal upon your arm," says the woman at the end (8:6). The point is not that by loving God we are enabled to love other human beings. The implication of the Song of Songs is the reverse: that by allowing ourselves to experience the passion and generosity of *human* love we learn what it means to be partners in *divine* love. Human eroticism, then, becomes no less than "the flame of Yahweh", the medium through which we learn to experience the passion that lies behind the universe.

But the Song of Songs has a particular importance for feminist theology. It seems to be the only text in the Bible which looks at love, sex and intimate relationships from the woman's point of view as much as the man's. The uninhibited companionship and the sense that she is an equal partner in the relationship make it a text that deserves closer study by contemporary women. The Shulamite has a sureness about her, and a confidence in her own power, which biblical women do not often have.

My work on AIDS in recent years has made me aware of the difficulties churches have in helping people to honour their own sexuality. Sexuality as such is something you leave behind when you come to church. From every part of the world, the story comes: that the church is quite adept at telling you what you should not do but is not of much use when it comes to affirming healthy eroticism. Sexuality then becomes a subject for guilt and secrecy, and eroticism comes to be associated with pornography, exploitation and other ways of relating which bear no resemblance to the model set out in the Song of Songs.

These difficulties have been exposed in recent years by the efforts many churches are making to respond to the AIDS pandemic. The most rapid increase in new infections is to be found among young women. An indication of the scale of the problem is that in many major cities of Sub-Saharan Africa, around 35 percent of women attending ante-natal clinics test positive for HIV. International agencies believe it is a matter of urgency that women take responsibility for protecting themselves against the virus. They cannot do this unless they are free to make their own sexual choices, without physical, economic or moral coercion; and that depends on being honest about the factors within cultures which prevent individuals from taking responsibility for their own sexuality.

On rational grounds, all this seems self-evident. But just as patriarchal cultures create the climate for an easy conscience about violent behaviour against women, so also they endorse sexual relationships in which women are expected to be either ignorant, compliant or both. Control is everything; and of course lesbian relationships, by definition, fall outside the bounds of masculine control. The relationship between patriarchy, women's sexuality and AIDS transmission is discussed extensively in my previous book, *Love in a Time of AIDS.*

Perhaps the saddest thing about the plight of Tina and all the others is that it is a denial of the individual's capacity to love – to love himself or herself, and to love others. Scholars have related the experience of human erotic passion described in Song of Songs to the passionate creativity of God, pointing out similarities between the Song of Songs and the first two chapters of Genesis. Look, for instance, at the joy God takes in Creation, the loving way in which details of the natural world are recorded. In her celebrated essay *The Use of the Erotic, the Erotic as Power,* the African American writer Audre Lorde argues that the erotic is the most powerful creative force in the world.

But it is a dangerous force, not because it rides roughshod over cultures, but because of the ease with which it can become corrupted or subverted into activity which has nothing to do with love at all. In a white man, say, it can easily become a form of collusion with oppression, rather than a release from it. In an article for *Auburn News* on the future of feminist theology, Kwok Pui-Lan writes:

> Asian women find it embarrassing to talk about sex and the erotic, not only because decent women are not supposed to raise those issues in public, but also because many of our sisters are working as prostitutes in the hotels, night-clubs, bars, disco-joints and cocktail lounges in the big cities like Manila, Bangkok, Taipei, Hong Kong and Seoul... The magnitude of the international flesh trade, and the courageous action of women's groups challenge us to rethink the connection between the language of the erotic, the control of the female body and power over women in its naked and symbolic forms.

In every culture, the social construction of sexuality tends to be heterosexual. Being in the category "heterosexual" is taken as a sign of psychic health. To use an image from the world of computers, heterosexuality can be described as the "default setting". Of course, heterosexual relationships in fact range from mutual support, commitment and delight to violent and oppressive exploitation of innocent persons. The same is true of homosexual relationships. But every computer user is aware of the tyranny of the "default setting". Heterosexual behaviour may be considered the only acceptable expression of sexuality, even though there is a wealth of evidence of its abuse. Conversely, same-sex relationships, which are rarely – perhaps never – the norm, are considered evidence of psychic damage, even though many are mutually supportive, loving and committed.

Of all the true-life sex-stories of recent times, President Bill Clinton's sexual acts with a young woman on his staff must be the best documented. "I did not have sexual relations with that woman," he told the world. *You're joking,* said the world, when it heard what he had actually done. The world's instinctive verdict is that if we are to think ethically about sex, it is not sex-as-action that we should focus on, it is sex-as-relationship. In the Song of Songs, the only "sexual act" which is named is a kiss. And yet there is no ambiguity about the passionate nature of the relationship itself. Furthermore, the Song of Songs repeatedly acknowledges the need to allow a relationship to set its own pace: *I adjure you, O daughters of Jerusalem..., do not stir up or awaken love until it is ready.* Force, coercion or the exploitation of an unequal power relationship are to be condemned. *My vineyard, my very own, is for myself,* says the Shulamite, who is therefore able to give herself freely to her love.

Sadly, it has become almost impossible to talk about sexuality at all in church circles these days, because the word itself has been so corrupted. "Sexuality" has come to mean "sexual orientation", which in itself is a euphemism for "heterosexual-and-homosexual", which leads into a political mine-field which all but the brave will avoid. Therefore we shroud the subject in silence, because the very language we need for discussing it offends against somebody's taboo. I would risk causing bitter offence to a lesbian woman from my own country if I were to suggest for one moment that there was anything odd about her sexual orientation. I would cause equal offence to a woman from a different culture by suggesting that it was "normal". There are times when "political correctness" results in a veil of silence and non-communication. The great blessing is that, in talking with Decade women as individuals, I met openness and an honest desire to understand more.

As human beings, we are built for relationships with each other, and that means sexual relationships as well as all the rest. I speak as a heterosexual woman. In claiming the right to be what I am, and to relate as I was created to relate, I must in the same breath acknowledge the right of others to do the same. If human passion is made of the same stuff as the divine energy which created the universe, then it is not for me to lock it up and label it "poison". If many waters cannot quench love, then it is not for me to pour contempt upon it. If I am to make judgments about the ways in which humans relate to each other, then it is by God's standards of love and fidelity and kindness, of self-sacrifice and unlimited compassion that I must do so.

Choosing the Better Part?

(Luke 10:38-42)

"I do not *believe* this!", exclaims Martha of Bethany furiously. Pushing the scroll to one side, she hobbles out of the little house to find her sister. She is so angry that she can hardly breathe.

"What ever is the matter?", asks Mary in astonishment. She straightens up, painfully, from her morning task of watering the vines. "I'm getting too old for this," she mutters.

"It's the Luke story," says Martha. "Have you read the parts where he talks about us? Or haven't you got that far yet?"[1]

"Why? What does he say?", enquires Mary. She picks up the water jar.

"Oh, *leave* that!", cries Martha. "Come inside and let me read it to you."

Inside, she picks up the scroll with shaking hands. "Remember how they all used to come here, and what fun it was? Remember how Jesus would talk, and we would tease him, and how everything seemed so much better when he was here? Well...," – she struggles for words – "Luke has written it all down, but not the way it was at all.

"Look," she says, jabbing at the text. "Here am I, supposed to be doing all the work, and here you are, sitting around listening. And then I go whining to ask *him* to tell you to help me. It was *never* like that. If I had wanted you to help, I would have told you myself.

"And he was our *friend,*" she continues, "not this... this *kyrios* figure.[2] And how does Luke *dare* to make it sound as if we bickered like that? Of course, it's not as bad for you. You are the one who can do no wrong, whereas I'm portrayed as someone who fusses around, too stupid to join in, and then complains because you are enjoying yourself." She looks at her sister with love.

Mary has now managed to read the passage for herself. "I don't know," she says. "I think I would rather be remembered as *you* are – getting on with things and being angry when you think things are not going right – rather than acting like one of those dumb women who sat at his feet and gazed into his eyes and never said a word. I mean, Luke has set us both up. Women are either housekeepers without a theological idea in their heads, or else they are a silent and adoring audience for a male teacher."

"But it wasn't like that," cries Martha passionately. "Jesus never made a distinction between us and the men. He treated us all equally. The author should have got his facts right, if he wanted to write about Jesus. Any number of people were guests in this house, and any of them could have told him the truth."

Mary is gazing thoughtfully at the scroll. "You know, the chapters I read were a bit like that," she says. "I mean, the author *seems* to be interested in women, but then it is as if he is only using what they have said or done as an opportunity for putting them down."

"Well, there is another part you should see, then," says Martha. "Go back a bit. There is a kind of theme sentence, introducing this part of the story. Look, it says: 'The twelve were with him, as well as some women who had been cured of evil spirits and infirmities: Mary, called Magdalene, from whom seven demons had gone out, and Joanna, the wife of Herod's steward Chuza, and Susanna, and many others, who provided for them out of their resources' (Luke 8:1-3). How about that? He shows the *men* as the in-group, and the *women* as either humble and grateful because they have been healed, or else as rich women with time on their hands. Those women were *running the show,* for goodness' sake. They were teaching and organizing, going to market and looking after the food and so on, and some of them were paying for it all as well." She pauses. "*Plus* all the social stigma of women trailing round the country with an itinerant preacher," she adds.

"Yes," comments Mary, "and I think the passage you just read is even worse than the one about us. At least when he talks about you and me, he seems to be saying that it is possible to choose. You can *either* be silent and adoring, *or* you can be practical and managing. In the other passage it sounds as if women have to be everything, and get no credit for it. Everything except leaders or proper disciples, of course."

For a moment the sisters are silent. "I have been try-ing to work out what Luke's real agenda is in this book," Martha says at last. "Because telling the story of Jesus *as it actually happened* is obviously not part of it."

"Well," says Mary, "just think who he is. He is trying to develop these house churches as part of the whole missionary project. What he wants is for the men to go around being missionaries, teaching and preaching, and the women to look after the house groups, and see that the whole thing runs smoothly. They will need the women – to open their houses for meetings and proba-bly to pay for it all. That is his real agenda. That is why he has described us in that way. He doesn't want women who are like us on board. He wants women who are either competent hostesses, or good listeners who don't interrupt. This book is not for us; it is for these new Chris-tians. What he has done is to write *our* story in such a way as to make it look as if that is how it was when Jesus was alive. He is hoping to persuade them that what they are doing now is what Jesus would have liked."

There is a long pause, while they remember. "We loved him so much," murmurs Mary. "And he loved us too, all of us. Remember the time I poured all that oint-ment on his feet? Remember when we thought Lazarus was dead? When you suddenly announced that he was the Christ and we all realized that it was true, and why had we not seen it before? I hope someone, sometime, manages to write it as it was."

Martha gets painfully to her feet, which is not as easy as it was when she was younger. "Well, if you're not going to do any work, I am!", she snaps. "But what I sim-ply cannot bear is the thought of all those women, down the ages, who will see themselves reflected in me, and feel completely furious at what Jesus is supposed to have said. Most of them will still be doing traditional women's things, I expect, like cooking and cleaning, and they will think he was being disparaging towards *them* as well, and dismissive about what *they* do. But they won't be able to *admit* that they are angry, because it was Jesus who said it – at least they will think it was – and being angry would mean being angry with *him,* which of course will not be allowed. So when women *do* choose to be thinkers and scholars in the future, or maybe just sit around and read, then the ones who are still bogged down in the traditional jobs will take out their hurt and fury on these others, because they feel they have had such a raw deal themselves.[3] So my story will just confuse people and make them cross, instead of being the story of the very best friendship that any woman ever had..."

Suddenly Martha runs out of steam. Mary reaches out and touches her arm. She knows when her sister is trying not to cry. "Well, *somebody* has to see to it that we will have grapes this year," mutters Martha crossly, and stomps off into the garden. Soon she is crouched among the young bushes, pouring water around their roots from the big earthen pot. All morning she has been keeping back the tears. But now, into the cracked red earth, she lets them flow unchecked. It needs the water, after all.

NOTES

[1] This Window, drawing on an interpretation of the Martha and Mary story in Elisabeth Schüssler Fiorenza's *But She Said...*, invites the reader to imagine that the two sisters have acquired a copy of Luke's gospel and are reading it. This gospel was probably written around 80-85 C.E., by which time Martha and Mary would have been extremely old, if not dead. Scholars believe the author came from Syrian Antioch. There is no evidence that the gospel was written by Luke the physician. R.J. Karris suggests it was addressed to "a primarily Gentile audience with well-to-do members who are painfully rethinking their missionary thrusts in a hostile environment".

[2] *Kyrios,* usually translated in English as "Lord", is the Greek term. Jesus-as-Kyrios is the centre of the action. Luke 10:38-42 is a story about Jesus, not about the two women. Schüssler Fiorenza points out that it is important for feminist interpreters of the gospels to recognize the influence of "kyriocentric" thinking.

[3] Schüssler Fiorenza points out that this dynamic has been exploited by conservative elements in the church, so that women who adopt more traditional roles within the church are co-opted into rejecting those who choose to study theology or move into other traditionally male spheres of activity.

7. Um Cântico Novo

Cantai ao senhor
Um cântico novo

Brazilian song based on Psalm 96

Not breaking up but breaking open

For Korean theologian Chung Hyun-Kyung, the years since 1991 have been ones of brokenness and transformation. Invited to address a plenary session on the theme of the WCC's assembly in Canberra in 1991 ("Come, Holy Spirit – renew the whole creation") she gave a memorably colourful presentation. For her, she said, the image of the Holy Spirit comes from the image of the East Asian goddess Kwan In, whose compassion for living beings who are suffering makes her stay in this world to help others to achieve enlightenment, instead of passing into Nirvana. "Perhaps," said Chung, "this might also be a feminine image of the Christ."

"I was so innocent then," she says now. "I thought, 'if I honour my experience, then people will honour me too.'" She was quite unprepared for the outcry which followed. In using feminine images from her own culture to open up the road to God, Chung was offending against the institutionally driven patriarchal system of beliefs which validates Christianity, both Western and Eastern, and also the Christianity of countries in the South which were formed by it. This version of Christianity has marketed God as a middle-class white male intellectual, who likes a lot of words but is easily shocked by anything that is spontaneously physical – apart from organized sport and legitimate hard work, of which he approves. This image has shaped the mindset of Christians, as well as the structures and liturgies of most churches. Entertain the possibility of a creative, erotic, female God, and the whole pack of cards might come crashing around one's ears.

In the years that followed the Canberra assembly, Chung Hyun-Kyung experienced theological violence, professional violence, personal violence. There were death threats. Korean Christians distributed leaflets saying "Kill the shaman! Kill the witch! Kill the heretic!" Her job became impossible and her marriage broke up. "Now I know how dangerous the world can be," she says.

A similar right-wing attack followed the Re-imagining Conference, held in the USA in 1993 in connection with the Ecumenical Decade. Here there was a celebration of Wisdom-Sophia, found in the deuterocanonical Book of Wisdom and elsewhere, and accepted by serious theologians as a biblical "type" for the Holy Spirit. But when the press got hold of the story, it was presented around the world as a mass movement of Christian women worshipping pagan goddesses. Organizers received death threats, and one of them, Mary Ann Lundy, was dismissed from her job with her church.

For a while, Chung Hyun-Kyung thought she was "breaking up". Now, instead, she sees in what has happened to her a process of "breaking open" in her own life. Being broken, she has found, is a pre-condition for healing. After the death-process – which was what her own experience felt like – one is not afraid of anything. The crucified woman becomes a resurrected goddess, "broken open" rather than "broken up" – and that is where healing can begin.

It is on healing that she now concentrates as a theologian. "You cannot be healed by standing still," she says. "The healing house for women is social change and movement. I want to be a healer *and* theologian, to be theologian *as* healer." To be healed, it is necessary to unlock within oneself the image of God, the God who loves and creates and is full of joy. Through the tears, she says, you can see the rainbow. It is heresy to imagine you can define God by dressing God in the clothes of patriarchy, or of any other particular culture. "The world is so big," she says. "God is so big."

In the Christian feminist movement, Chung believes, too much energy has been spent on complaining *to* men and complaining *about* men. At this turning of the millennium, change is in the air, with the pressure coming especially from young women. She compares feminist theology to fire; it is hugely liberating, not just for women but for everyone. If the churches can accept feminist theology, then the "mainstream theology" of the next century will be different. Chung quotes the Sufi mystic Rumi: "At the end, your rusty chain will turn into a necklace of gold." The future can be really fun, really beautiful, really inclusive.

Claiming the story

Broken open by the past, Chung Hyun-Kyung sees herself as now poised on the threshold of the golden future. A bird of paradise herself, in beautiful dramatic clothes, she insists on the importance of glamour and movement and colour in her presentations. In the last ten years, her story has moved the story of the ecumenical women's movement forward. But just what is that story? And who are its heroines and heroes?

The large and ambitious Her-story exhibition, launched in Harare, sets out that history as it has unfolded over the past fifty years. It has hundreds of photographs of women who have contributed to the movement, their writings and an honour roll of women whose names do not appear on the panels. This is essential data for the movement's self-understanding, and for its ability to claim its own role-models and saints.

Further data comes from the WCC's study of the Community of Women and Men in the Church (1978-1981), which generated some highly original thinking and writing in the areas of anthropology and ecclesiology. And more recently the mid-Decade team visits produced a wealth of data, and the scriptural focus of the Decade encouraged much creative biblical work. *Living Letters* and other publications give some idea of its flavour and its major themes. In putting together "the story", these are vital source materials.

But 1948 was not the beginning of history. The tale of women's determination to take their place in the unfolding story of God's purposes for creation goes back to the beginning of Judaeo-Christian history. Who then are our saints and role models? What are our founding myths? Eve, in risking everything for understanding, was the first offender against patriarchy. She is our first role-model. Hagar, the great survivor, finds springs of water in the wilderness and the promise from The God Who Sees that she and her descendants are part of the plans which that God has for this world. The Shulamite woman claims her right to a passionate sexual relationship in which she enjoys the freedom to decide whether or not to give herself. The Virgin Mary has become the subject of a whole new school of feminist theology. And so on. In re-exploring these characters, it would be good also to honour some of the many men who, over the long span of history, have stood beside women and believed their testimonies.

As Christian women, these characters are part of our history: a history which – no less than the history of the indigenous peoples described by Olivia Juarez in Chapter 5 – is in urgent need of reclaiming from its patriarchal prison. In her excellent feminist theological reading of the communion of saints, US Catholic theologian Elizabeth A. Johnson claims that we should look on our foremothers and forefathers, the "saints" of our own tradition, as "an inclusive community of friends of God and prophets, rather than a spiritual hierarchy of patrons and petitioners." They are part of our own story. She quotes from John Haught's *The Promise of Nature:*

> If we are unable to symbolize immortality in one way or another, we lose any sense of relatedness to the vast world that has gone before us, as well as to the generations of living beings that may follow. In breaking our connection with other generations, we understandably forfeit our responsibility to them. Stranded in a meaninglessly brief life span, and severed from communion with the perished past or the promised future, we grow ethically impotent.

In practice, this work is being done by feminist historians and theologians in all regions. Nevertheless, the WCC's experience over fifty years has generated some rich data and its network of related organizations and institutions is worldwide. Thus it would seem that the Council has a huge potential contribution to make to the process of reclaiming our past.

Unravelling the garment

What then is this promised future to hold – this "golden necklace" into which our "rusty chain" is to be transformed?

In all parts of the world, access to theological education has been seen as a key to the advancement of women in the churches. Without it, the scope of women's participation is necessarily limited, and roles that involve preaching, teaching or study are closed.

Lisa-Meo, from Fiji, is co-ordinator of Women in Theological Education in the South Pacific (WITE). The South Pacific Association of Theological Schools has responded to the Decade by giving WITE a mandate to advocate for women in theological education. The problem is that while churches acknowledge the right of women to study theology if they wish, the schools of theology are oriented towards ordination, which is only open to men. What is the point of educating women in theology, they ask, when there is no role available to them at the end of the process? The clergy at the moment flatly oppose the idea of lay leadership, although there is no logical reason why this should demand ordained status. Theological education, says Lisa, should be a means of liberation, not just a form of vocational training. Now there is talk of setting up a school of theology at the University of the South Pacific, which could provide an opportunity to set theological studies on the same footing as other academic disciplines.

Ofelia Ortega is principal of the Ecumenical Theological College in Matanzas, Cuba. From 1988 to 1997 she was responsible for the WCC's work with theological education in Central America and the Caribbean. She says that the annual women's seminars organized since 1985 by the WCC's Ecumenical Institute in Bossey have changed her life. She came to realize that theological education is not just one thing. It must relate to the cultures of different church structures, different liturgical frameworks, different regions. Orthodox women have their own seminars, exploring feminist imagery in icons and liturgy.

Recent years have seen the establishment of continental or regional networks to monitor and promote the cause of women in theological education. The South Pacific network is one of these, as is the influential Circle of Concerned African Women Theologians. The Latin America network is based in Costa Rica, but works at sub-regional level on the sharing of resources. In the South, says Ofelia Ortega, no one ever does theology on their own: it is a group activity, which is not necessarily done in theological colleges. You go to the people, like liberation theologian Elsa Tamez, who travels to hold seminars with indigenous women; or like *mujerista* theologian Ada Maria Isasi-Diaz, who works with communities of Latino women in the USA.

It is difficult to over-estimate the importance of this movement. In Latin America, "doing women's theology" brought together the popular movements with academics and theologians, and became an influential bottom-up movement which genuinely succeeded in moving the agenda along in theological colleges, resulting in the appointment of women staff, and the adoption of feminist theology and gender studies on the curricula of Protestant colleges, like the ecumenical theological institute ISEDET, in Buenos Aires. Among the fine women theologians in Brazil are Wanda Deifelt, who teaches theology in the Lutheran Seminary in Sao Leopoldo and who gave one of the addresses on the theme at the Harare assembly, and Nancy Pereira Cardoso, who teaches biblical studies at the Roman Catholic Sao Paolo Institute. With its programme of ecumenical theological education, the Latin American Council of Churches (CLAI) has monitored the process of empowering women.

Several times I have mentioned that the majority of "mainstream" theology and biblical interpretation has been written by men working in the context of patriarchal organizations and cultures. Many candidates for ordination may go through their entire training without once having a serious theological discussion with a woman. Students in university schools of theology may never be taught by a woman member of staff. Where courses in feminist theology are included in the curriculum, they are often not compulsory, and may therefore be attended only by women.

Meanwhile, women in all parts of the world are working to develop new ways of interpreting the scriptures. They are introducing women's resources and experiences into pastoral studies courses, developing new liturgies and adapting old ones, bringing their own spiritual insights to bear on matters of prayer, spiritual direction and relationships generally.

This movement has many friends among male pastors and theologians. Without these, nothing could have been achieved. Nevertheless, the *overall* response of the male-stream academic establishment is either to try to co-opt (and therefore control) feminist theology, or else to discredit it. A third group may accept the thinking, even respect it for its originality and insights, but experience acute discomfort with the anger which sometimes goes with it. In feminist circles, a debate is in progress. Having achieved some kind of autonomy within academic institutions, should feminist theologians now be joining with mainstream, male-stream theology and trying to change its language and orientation? Or will that result in a sacrifice of what has been achieved so far, and in becoming a footnote to the dominant theological paradigm? If that is the case, then the answer is to go on fighting for more academic posts and research grants for feminist theologians who will continue to develop hermeneutical methods and principles which are distinctively women's, while being aware that this lays them open to the charge that their prime motivation comes from politically inspired radical feminism, and not from a passionate search for the truth.

I would say two things in response. One is that the best feminist theology in every part of the world is not just original, but also rigorously argued and profoundly orthodox in the way it honours source material, contemporary scholarship and context. The second is that the above problematic is absolutely inescapable. There is no right answer. Of course it is to be hoped that feminist insights will begin to colour the work and the hermeneutical methods of male-stream theology. Women's theology will otherwise remain a splinter group, focusing women's energies and channelling their experience into by-waters where they can do no harm. On the other hand, it is a young discipline which is developing traditions and hermeneutical practices which are both controversial and have important implications for other marginalized groupings within the churches. The true challenge for feminists is then to make the discipline itself more broadly relevant to the lives of women outside the world of academic theology, and then to draw these women into a conversation that will help them to realize that they too can do theology, and that the Christian God is a God who honours women's experience, even if this is not immediately clear from the way the church has read the canon of scriptural writings it has handed down to us.

In seeking to unravel the garments of patriarchy, the most obvious thread to pull may appear to be the thread of activism. In fact, however, it may be the thread of consciousness and the thread of theological validation that we should be worrying at. For its member churches – and for the Roman Catholic Church, with its many distinguished feminist theologians – the World Council may seem to be ideally placed to provide a safe and inclusive space for this theological and spiritual "thread-worrying" to happen.

Irja Askola, from Finland, was responsible until recently for the women's and inter-church service desks at the Conference of European Churches. "Feminist theology changed my life," she says. "It gave language to my feelings. Traditional theology confirms dualism. Feminist theology brings together heart and mind. It is no longer either/or. What feminist theology has to offer to the world is the opportunity to be fully alive."

Resisting the culture of silence

A lawyer and a mother from Chicago, Ann Glynn-Mackoul is a member of the Greek Orthodox Church. She does some work for the Greek Orthodox Patriarchate of Antioch and all the East.

When I met her in Harare, she was unhappy and anxious. She loved being at the Decade Festival, she said. She was moved by the sense of women gathered for a common purpose, and in particular by the sessions on violence, the litany of "Your story is my story, your story is our story." She said the most difficult thing she has ever had to do was to get up during the plenary session at the WCC assembly and publicly dissociate herself from the final letter sent by Festival participants to the assembly delegates.

Most of the letter was fine, she said, particularly its statements on violence and its insights into cultures of silence. But the final draft contained comments which had not been shared in the plenary. The phrase which had "sneaked in without anyone having a chance to object" was "reproductive rights": a phrase which "is dynamite in the USA". It is vitally important for Orthodox attitudes to the WCC that it should *not* be seen to be "pro-abortion".

"The development of theology that starts with contemporary problems is foreign to Orthodox tradition," says Ann Glynn-Mackoul. "In our icons we see the Mother of God at the foot of the cross. Our stories are of earthly struggles which we recognize as spiritual struggles. We are not used to doing theology in this way."

In media reports of the Festival and the assembly, those few issues which cause division among the churches drew far more attention than the many issues which unite them. It is a painful reality that the ecclesial cultures in which some churches are rooted make it very difficult for them to stay within the fold, and the participation of women is one particularly problematic factor. Most would not go as far as to describe the use of inclusive language in liturgy as "blasphemous", as one Russian Orthodox assembly delegate did. But it is clear that within an overall commitment to openness, justice and mutual collaboration, there is a wide diversity in terms of actual policies and arrangements. On this spectrum, churches which ordain women bishops are at one end, and churches where women are only just struggling into positions of lay participation are at the other. Being in solidarity with women from different situations means standing alongside them while they fight their own battles, and not assuming that one's own solutions are the correct ones for everyone, even if they are the solutions favoured by the majority.

It was sad that Ann Glynn-Mackoul felt she had to dissociate herself from the statement coming from the Festival. For the organizers, it was a body-blow from which they have not yet fully recovered. But she must be honoured for her refusal to be sucked into the "culture of silence" which could have driven a lesser woman to keep quiet.

"Um cântico novo"

In these chapters we have listened to many voices, past and present, biblical and contemporary, which claim to be heard. What then is the "new song" for the new millennium?

First, there are the cries of those in pain: women and girls who are abused and battered, bought and sold for sex; women living with the violence of racism; women who see their children waste and die, because of the economic violence of debt and corruption and the mismanagement of resources; women whose homes are bombed, whose fields are sown with land-mines made in far-off countries where large profits are made from arms sales; women dying of AIDS or giving birth to infected children because they have no way of setting the terms of their own sexual encounters; women who are silenced and disregarded within the church, and told that this is the will of God. This must surely be the first stanza of our song, the first concern of any group which seeks to take the agenda further.

Then there is the song of the world. Globalization is more than just economics. Over a hundred years ago, Samuel Morse became an apostle of globalization when he tapped into his newly invented telegraph machine the message "What hath God wrought?". The message is still hanging in the air around our planet. Globalization is bringing about technological, ecological, political and cultural change in all parts of the world. From the outside, family, work, tradition, government, industry may look much the same, but inside they have changed. The globalization of systems is paralleled by the emergence from below of a global civil society and global movements within it. Among them are changes in patterns of family life, and the increasing participation of women in public life. Globalization, says the radical economist Anthony Giddens, is inside us: and it is the key to the new consciousness of women. So our second stanza must combine a rejection of the forces of economic, political and ecological exploitation which globalization permits, with a celebration of its vision of the one world which can bring us together in solidarity.

Stanza three is the song of diversity. It is tempting to write this as a song of celebration and adventure, a kind of Decade Festival set to music. Beneath the rejoicing, however, there is the constant threat of discord and violence. This is perhaps the most difficult stanza to orchestrate, because it means allowing the tune to sing while always recognizing its potential for sliding into disharmony.

Then there is the song of the wilderness. Prophets live in the wilderness, because until you stand outside the system you are unable to see clearly what is happening within it. Those who seek to change structures and cultures may find that they have to go into the wilderness to do it. While they are there, like Hagar, they learn about loneliness, they learn about pain, but they also learn about survival, they learn that there is living water to be found even in the most unlikely places. So our fourth stanza contains the cry of loneliness and fear which is an inescapable part of the wilderness experience, but it ends on the crescendo of surprise and delight which comes when you find that God is there before you.

Stanza five opens with firmness and clarity. Beneath it, though, there is weariness. It is the song of the women who have made it into positions of power. We have to be so many things, they say. We must be role models for women, but fight our corner in a man's world. We must be loyal to the institutions we serve, but keep faith with our longing for change. We have left the safety of the ranks, but we are aliens, still, in the corridors of power. We are tired. *We are lonely...* The music falters, then grows strong again. We are lonely, yes: but we are here, *and we are staying...*

The next stanza has a chorus of male voices in the background. It is the song of the young women. With the bass part added, the harmony is richer and fuller. This is the song of community, the song of companionship, the song of giving and taking. Men are not the enemy, it says, though some men are – and some women too. We can sing and dance together and all will not be lost. Do not create a matriarchy which is a mirror image of patriarchy. Know your beauty, says the song: you can afford to be lovely, as well as articulate and intelligent. It is no longer the "churches in solidarity with women", because women *are* the church. If you put yourselves on the margins, says the song, then that is where you will be. And *why* are you always so angry? That is the sixth stanza.

The seventh and final stanza is the song of the living water. The music runs away from us, in long, liquid cadences. A new voice joins in now: warm, and half familiar, a voice we know but cannot place. The urgency increases. "Enjoy the living water," says the song; "but remember that it is given you in trust. My church is not for itself, it is for those outside itself. My living water is for you to pass on to others, for the life of my world."

Like the best of songs, this song leads into with another story.

Living Water

(John 4:1-42)

It is almost midday: too hot to be carrying water, too late in the day to meet the other women, too early for the courting couples. Mira rests for a moment by the well. A man is there, quietly sitting. A *Jew.* Irritation floods over her. How she loathes them, with their arrogance and their condescension, their rigid religious laws, their contempt for her people. *Ignore him,* she mutters. Not that there is much need: as a woman and a Samaritan, he will never bother her. She reaches for the rope and the iron hook.

"Why don't you give me a drink?", says a voice behind her.

Mira turns around, astonished. "How is it that you come begging to me, a woman of Samaria?", she asks.[1]

"If you knew who I am, it would be living water we were talking about, and you would be begging *me* to give it to *you,*" answers the stranger calmly.

Not just a Jew, she thinks, *but a crazy one, too.* "Oh yes?", she says. "And just how would you have done that? Our forefather Jacob gave us this well, and even he needed a water jar, which you do not have."

"But my water is different," the Jew persists. "You will never be thirsty again if you drink my water. It will become like a spring of water, overflowing to eternal life."

Oh, for goodness' sake, she thinks, pulling up the bucket with her strong arms. But it does not pay to annoy them. "Fine," she says, humouring him. "Give me some of your water, and I will never need to come to this well again." She has learned the hard way about the dangers of going for water on your own, about how men behave towards lone women. Against her better judgment, however, she is beginning to enjoy this strange conversation. All the same. *Best not to get too involved,* she thinks. *Just keep him talking till you have finished, and then go.*

It is as if he has read her mind. "Why don't you go and fetch your husband", says the Jew, "and then come back and talk to me?"

She loses her grip on the rope, then catches it again as the bucket swings. *What is this?*, she thinks. But he seems harmless enough, if a bit mad. "I have no husband...," she says cautiously, looking at him closely for the first time. Surely he cannot be *laughing* at her?

"Quite so," he says dryly. "You have had five men, and the one you live with now is not your husband."[2]

Mira goes cold. The bucket slips from her hands. Who *is* this man? *And how does he know?* Under the law of Jews and Samaritans, a woman cannot divorce a man. But a man can divorce a woman for almost any reason, childlessness being the commonest.[3] Social isolation she knows about: that is the penalty for being abandoned. For adultery, though, you can be stoned to death. *Just change the subject*, she thinks, swallowing her panic. *Chat about anything...* "I can see you are a real prophet, sir," she says conversationally. "Then you will know that our ancestors worshipped God on this holy mountain. But you, I think, believe that God can be worshipped only in Jerusalem."

Before the words are out of her mouth, she realizes how inappropriate they are. *They* never talk about religion with women.

But this extraordinary person seems to take her seriously. "Soon," he replies, "the time will come when you will not need a special place to worship. No temple, no holy mountain. The time is coming – in fact the time has already come – when true worshippers will worship the Father in spirit and in truth. The Father is longing for such as these to worship him. God is spirit, so those who really worship him must do so in spirit, and also in truth."

Truth. How she has longed to live in the truth, to be accepted for what she is. How she has dreamed about the Messiah whom Moses promised to her people, fantasized about the moment when he would come and set her free from her burden of rejection and exclusion, the load she is destined to carry for the rest of her life. "I know that the Messiah is coming," she says carefully. "I know that when he comes he will tell us everything." With a wild hope, which feels almost like trust, she turns to face him. She sees humour, warmth, kind eyes, transparent goodness. His presence enfolds her.

"Well, you are talking with him now," says the man. "I am the Messiah."

At that moment, a group of men comes round the corner, stopping in astonishment when they see their friend in conversation with a woman. A *Samaritan* woman, too... They are dumbstruck, but she knows what they are thinking as clearly as if they have shouted it aloud. Mira puts down her water jar. "Here, drink this," she says to him, and stumbles down the road towards the city.

What has she done, leaving her only jar with a stranger? The neighbours, dozing in the midday sun, look up in astonishment as she catapults headlong into the familiar street. "Is somebody chasing you, Mira?", shouts a voice.

Breathlessly, she stops. "You have to come!", she gasps. "There is this man by Jacob's well who told me everything I have ever done!"

"What, everything?" Laughter ripples around the little group.

"No, I mean it!", she cries. "He sees everything; he knows the truth, but he doesn't condemn. He is a Jew, but he is not like a Jew. He says you don't have to be in the temple to worship God. He says God is longing for all those who love truth to come and worship him. Surely" – she pauses – "he cannot really be the Messiah, can he? Because that's who he says he is. Come on, come and see him, before he goes."

One by one, sleepy with heat, they struggle to their feet. Something about her urgency, her sincerity, tells them that what she is saying is true. Intrigued, the little procession follows her back to the well. "Let him still be there," she prays. "Let them believe him."

And there he is, still: talking to the other men she saw, who are looking hot, mystified and rather cross. "Another four months till the harvest?", he is saying. "Just look around and see how the fields are ripe for harvesting." He has seen her coming with the others.

*   *   *

Mira never forgot the next days: how Jesus and the disciples stayed with them in Sychar for two days, how the people hung onto his words, how from that time on the community of his followers grew among the people of Samaria. "It is no longer because of what you said that

120

we believe," they told her. "It is because we have met him and heard him for ourselves, and we know he is the Saviour."

Mira always remembered his words to her before he left. Years later, lingering by Jacob's well in the cool of the evening, she would have a sudden sense of his closeness. "Others reaped," he is saying gently, "but you were the one who sowed the seed. It was because of your testimony that they first believed."[4]

Which of course is true. She picks up the old jar and sets off down the path. Water is life. It is tears, it is cleaning; it is baptism, it is an end to thirst. It is heavy. *He and his living water,* she thinks. Living water, waters of life... *He gave me so much...* He looked into her heart and saw what was there, and because of that she was able to bring her own people to this new sense of happiness and community.

Tonight he seems very close. "He gave me back my life," she thinks. "I gave him water from Jacob's Well, but what he gave to me was living water." *Living water...* It is still flowing, swelling, trickling into her body, her head, her spirit, overflowing into the quiet, warm evening, gushing up to eternal life, further and further, until the whole created universe is flooded.

Mira shakes herself. It is time to stop dreaming. There is work to be done. It is almost as if he has fallen into step beside her on the rocky path. Anyway, the bucket seems much lighter.

For there is no more this race and that mountain,
No more Jew or Samaritan, no male nor female here,
Only Truth and Spirit are in the ripe fields,
Awaiting the harvest.

Musa Dube

NOTES

1 Since Samaritan women were believed to be ritually unclean, it would have been unthinkable for a Jewish man to ask anything of a Samaritan woman.
2 Some scholars have suggested that John was relating the woman to the land of Israel, with the five husbands referring to Israel's frequent occupations by foreign powers.
3 Jewish regulations about adultery applied in Samaritan law. The most likely reason for this woman to have had a number of husbands would not be promiscuity but an inability to have children, which allowed a man to desert his wife for another.
4 This is a key missiological text, and the first missionary is a woman. The people of Sychar came to meet Jesus "because of her testimony", but it was their personal experience of him that made them Christians.

Bibliography

Wesley Ariarajah, *Did I Betray the Gospel? The Letters of Paul and the Place of Women*, Geneva, WCC, 1996.

John Barton, ed., *The Cambridge Companion to Biblical Interpretation,* Cambridge, Cambridge U.P., 1998.

Maria Clara Lucchetti Bingemer, "Jesus Christ", in William R. Farmer, et al., ed., *The International Bible Commentary*, Collegeville MN, Liturgical Press, 1998.

David Bosch, *Transforming Mission: Paradigm Shifts in Theology of Mission*, Maryknoll NY, Orbis, 1991.

Raymond Brown, *Introduction to the New Testament*, New York, Doubleday, 1998.

Raymond Brown et al., eds, *The New Jerome Biblical Commentary*, Englewood Cliffs NJ, Prentice Hall, 1990; London, Cassell, 1989.

Beth Dominguez, "Women and the Bible: An Asian Perspective", in V. Fabella and D. Martinez, eds, *The Oaxtepec Encounter*, Port Harcourt, Nigeria, Ecumenical Association of Third World Theologians, 1986.

Rosemary Edet, "New Roles, New Challenges for African Women", in *ibid.*

Elisabeth Schüssler Fiorenza, *In Memory of Her: A Feminist Theological Reconstruction of Christian Origins*, New York, Crossroad, 1983.

Elisabeth Schüssler Fiorenza, *But She Said: Feminist Practices of Biblical Interpretation*, Boston, Beacon, 1992.

Ivone Gebara and Maria Clara Bingemer, *Mary: Mother of God, Mother of the Poor*, Maryknoll NY, Orbis, and London, Burns and Oates, 1989.

Aruna Gnanadason, *No Longer a Secret: The Church and Violence against Women*, Geneva, WCC, 1993, rev. ed. 1997.

Aruna Gnanadason, "The Church in Solidarity with Women: Utopia or Symbol of Faithfulness?", in Elisabeth Schüssler Fiorenza and M. Shawn Copeland, eds, *Feminist Theology in Different Contexts* (*Concilium*, 1996/1), Maryknoll NY, Orbis, and London, SCM, 1996.

Teresia M. Hinga, "Between Colonialism and Inculturation: Feminist Theologies in Africa", in *ibid.*

John Haught, *The Promise of Nature*, New York, Paulist, 1993.

Ada Maria Isasi-Diaz, *In the Struggle: Elaborating a Mujerista Theology*, Minneapolis, Fortress, 1993.

Ada Maria Isasi-Diaz, "Biblical Exegesis", in *The International Bible Commentary*.

Elizabeth A. Johnson, *Friends of God and Prophets: A Feminist Theological Reading of the Communion of Saints*, London, SCM, 1998.

Musimbi R.A. Kanyoro and Nyambura J. Njoroge, eds, *A Decade of Solidarity with the Bible*, Geneva, WCC, 1998.

Karen L. King, ed., *Images of the Feminine in Gnosticism*, Philadelphia, Fortress, 1988.

Ursula King, ed., *Feminist Theology from the Third World*, Maryknoll NY, Orbis, 1989.

Kwok Pui-Lan, "Discovering the Bible in the Non-Biblical World", *Semeia*, vol. 47, 1989, pp.30-40.

Kwok Pui-Lan, "The Future of Feminist Theology: An Asian Perspective", in *Auburn News*, 1992.

Living Letters: A Report on the Visits to the Churches during the Ecumenical Decade – Churches in Solidarity with Women, Geneva, WCC, 1997.

Audre Lorde, *Sister Outsider*, Trumansburg NY, Crossings Press, 1984.

Cullen Murphy, *The Word According to Eve*, London, Allen Lane, 1998.

Mercy Oduyoye, *Who Will Roll the Stone Away? The Ecumenical Decade of the Churches in Solidarity with Women*, Geneva, WCC, 1990.

Mercy Oduyoye, *The Daughters of Anowa: African Women and Patriarchy*, Maryknoll NY, Orbis, 1995.

Teresa Okure, "St John's Gospel", in *The International Bible Commentary*.

Teresa Okure, "Women in the Bible: An Africa Woman's Perspective", in *The Oaxtepec Encounter*, EATWOT, 1986.

Douglas M. Parrott, ed., *The Gospel of Mary*, Leiden, E.J. Brill, 1988.

124

Gillian Paterson, *Love in a Time of AIDS*, Geneva, WCC, 1995, and Maryknoll NY, Orbis, 1996 (Orbis title: *Women in the Time of AIDS*).

Carrie Pemberton, unpublished doctoral thesis for Cambridge University on the Circle of Concerned African Women Theologians.

Konrad Raiser, *To Be the Church: Challenges and Hopes for a New Millennium*, Geneva, WCC, 1997.

Carla Ricci, *Mary Magdalen and Many Others: Women who Followed Jesus*, Minneapolis, Augsburg-Fortress, 1994.

Letty M. Russell, *Church in the Round: Feminist Interpretation of the Church*, Philadelphia, Westminster/John Knox, 1993.

Sun Ai Park, "Emerging Women's Spirituality", in *The Oaxtepec Encounter*, EATWOT, 1986.

Elsa Tamez, *Through Her Eyes: Women's Theology from Latin America*, Maryknoll NY, Orbis, 1989.

Elsa Tamez, "Women's Re-reading of the Bible", in *The Oaxtepec Encounter*, EATWOT, 1986.

Phyllis Trible, *Texts of Terror: Literary-Feminist Readings of Biblical Narratives*, Philadelphia, Fortress, 1984.